CAPITALISM

STUDIES IN CONTEMPORARY POLITICS **ⅾⱷ**

Capitalism
Economic Individualism to Today's Welfare State

Communism
From Marx's *Manifesto* to 20th-century Reality

Socialism
Its Theoretical Roots and Present-day Development

By James D. Forman

Studies in Contemporary Politics offer wide-perspective examinations of major political and economic aspects of today's changing world. Using historical experience as a background, these books bring readers new understanding of the contemporary political scene.

STUDIES IN CONTEMPORARY POLITICS

CAPITALISM

Economic Individualism to Today's Welfare State

James D. Forman

Franklin Watts, Inc.   New York ● 1972

Library of Congress Cataloging in Publication Data

Forman, James D
    Capitalism.

    (Studies in contemporary politics)
    Bibliography: p.
    1. Capitalism—History. I. Title.
HC51.F63   330.12′2′09   72-6739
ISBN 0-531-02570-5

For John Donner.
I wish only that he could read it.

Contents

CAPITALISM

Capitalism Defined

Not since religious faith set men against each other in the wars of the sixteenth and seventeenth centuries has the world been so dominated by embattled ideologies as it is today. Communism, an eccentric theory in the nineteenth century, became a working reality with the First World War. Socialism, its democratic cousin, gained world importance with the second. In violent reaction, militant fascism arose from the bloody chaos left by the first war and sank with the shipwreck of the second. Just as the fascist system was a negative response to the political-economic systems endorsed by communism and socialism, so they had both emerged as alternatives to something older, capitalism.

Unlike its recent rivals, capitalism was born, not made. Without benefit of disgruntled intellectuals or revolutionaries, it simply grew as a way of doing business and, ultimately, as a way of living. There have been economists and philosophers to describe its workings, but it has developed in a pragmatic rather than a theoretical fashion.

3

Briefly, this economic system called capitalism, or free enterprise, or, euphemistically, economic humanism, is one in which the ownership of land and natural wealth, production, distribution, and exchange of goods, employment and reward for human labor are all entrusted to private rather than public control. A capitalist is anyone who has accumulated wealth that he employs not for immediate enjoyment but for the purpose of business investment, to produce goods and services, the income from which may in turn be used for enjoyment or for the further amassing of capital. The business enterprise may be managed by an individual, or, more commonly today, by a corporation. Free competition among capitalists in the marketplace is relied upon to keep business brisk and to maintain the buying public in a position to obtain the best available products at the most favorable prices.

The alternative to free competition is monopoly. A monopoly may occur naturally when one competitor, by fair means or foul, absorbs all competition and becomes the sole source of a certain product or service. Once this status is achieved, the public is deprived of choice and may be treated to high prices and shoddy goods without any alternative. Aware of this potential danger, democratic governments have created laws to thwart monopoly.

Monopoly achieved deliberately through the use of state power is the hallmark of the rival ideologies of communism and socialism, but even in this respect there are profound differences between the two. Having more faith in the state than in the individual, both seek to place the means of production in the hands of the government, and the result is a form of state capitalism. Communism, however, has achieved this result by revolution and violence and has maintained its economic monopoly by threat of force. Democratic socialism, on the other hand, has insisted upon methods of persuasion, and its successes have come by way of popular election.

Fascism arose as a nationalistic response to the two supranational socialistic movements, and domestic capitalism was feverishly encouraged by the Fascists in the beginning. The final economic result of fascism was a most unsatisfactory compromise in which the state assumed more and more power and gradually imposed an artificial capitalist monopoly in which the lesser capitalists were put out of business or made subservient, while the major businesses became strictly answerable to the government.

Capitalism was originally simply a name for an economic system of free enterprise. It was presumed to exist apart from politics. Though it has achieved its most impressive results under a democratic government, it has struggled along subject to the opposite political pole, totalitarian fascism. Today capitalism is evolving quickly, not only as an economic but as a sociopolitical system. These changes are in large measure a response to its rivals, socialism and communism, which aspire to embrace the complete society and, in so doing, have forced capitalism to assume a larger context. One name for the contemporary political-social development in capitalist countries is the welfare state. For balance and for contrast with the totalitarian fascist form of capitalism, it will here be called democratic capitalism.

This form of capitalism began its great development in eighteenth-century Britain and came of age with the spreading of the Victorian empire upon which the sun never set. Two world wars and a depression, however, have consumed that empire and left Britain experimenting with socialism. The center of capitalist development has moved elsewhere, and capitalism has endured vast changes and will endure many more. It remains the predominant economic system in the world, and in its two-hundred-year history it has brought about more progress than took place in all the centuries of bare subsistence that preceded it. Despite its embittered critics who speak of the downtrodden and exploited workers and peasants, capitalism has put the phrase "standard of living" into the vocabulary where "level of survival" might more accurately have fit before, and, in the United States of the twentieth century, democratic capitalism represents a height of economic power, wealth, and social well-being previously the stuff of dreams. Far from dead, democratic capitalism has withstood the onslaught of socialism, which came armed by the fear and despair of depression and world war. Even in the Communist countries, the spirit of free enterprise, particularly among artisans and farmers, is far from extinquished.

Though never stronger than now, capitalism has changed greatly in its two hundred years of life. Many, some eagerly, others with regret, have predicted its demise. Some characterize it as altered beyond recognition. In spite of all the changes of the past, the capitalistic system of today cannot be considered permanent and unchanging. Taking the facts of history as a starting point, and using the American experience as a pattern, the purpose here is to review democratic capitalism: its acknowledged past, productive if sometimes ruthless; its rapidly evolving and most controversial present; and the leading prognoses regarding its unknowable but all-important future.

The Beginning of Capitalism

For the ancient Greeks, economics was a matter of house-keeping, *oikonomikos,* from which our modern word derives. The basic speculations of the Greeks were not enlarged on by the Romans, for whom economics was a function of military conquest. With the eventual failure of this armed economy and the decline of the Roman Empire, intellectual speculation was taken over by Christian philosophers and theologians, who regarded economics as a moral question. Saint Thomas Aquinas set down some very definite rules, particularly regarding the "just price." The just price of any object offered for sale was to represent the cost of production plus a normal margin to sustain the seller's customary standard of living. Any more was sinful, as was also the exaction of interest on borrowed money. The theologians regarded money as a nonproductive medium of exchange, and the charging of any interest was, by definition, usury. The objection was more than ethical or religious. The medieval church and the feudal lords correctly foresaw a threat to their security in the growth of capitalism. None yet had a name for such market activity, but the new emphasis on the condemnation of usury was a symptom that the feudal order was being undermined by new ways of carrying on exchange and production.

Feudal Economics   Thus Saint Thomas Aquinas and his followers, called the Schoolmen, insisted on the just price as the basis of any economic transaction, and he who dealt sharply was in danger of hellfire. This moral attitude tended to limit market activity up until the fifteenth century. The basis for political authority was divine right, and rulers governed by the grace of God. All obligations and privileges were divinely ordained and, as in ancient Greece and Rome, property was held by a limited class in return for military services. At the economic base of this feudal pyramid were the serfs, an agricultural population that provided labor to produce food for their lord in return for his protection against attack. The economy was almost solely agricultural and localized. Travel, a word derived from the same root as *travail,* was difficult and dangerous. Each manorial estate consumed most of what its serfs produced.

Only gradually, as Europe became more orderly, did commerce by land and sea become a practical risk. Surplus crops could be sold or, more often, bartered for other products. Towns and cities began to grow while merchants gradually prospered. The older order and its strictly moralistic economy began to break down, although this change did not happen overnight. In England, the absolute power of the king was first formally limited in 1215 by the Magna Carta, a victory for the barons and an indication of political adaptation.

Meanwhile, the real revolution proceeded quietly and slowly. Agricultural methods improved, and food surpluses developed. Populations increased. Towns began to flourish, and then cities, as centers of commercial exchange. Control by clergy and nobility was for the first time threatened by the businessman, a fact bemoaned by the English friar Roger Bacon, who railed against greedy sheepmongers and graziers. The old pattern of people born to a fixed place and fulfilling a set life function was passing. Peasants, freed of the restraints of serfdom, moved to the cities or, when they could afford to, began to pay money rent in lieu of services to their lord. The rent served the lord well in buying a greater variety of goods than the peasant could supply. As rents increased, peasants had to adapt their crops toward marketable products. Traders multiplied. Competition developed between towns and the towns grew wealthy. Kings began to discover that money derived from taxing this new commerce was one way to purchase an army, a more reliable army than one made up of a band of jealous nobles and their followers.

World Commerce Along with local socioeconomic changes, the international scene was evolving. The ninth and tenth centuries had marked a low ebb in international trade, for it had been a period of great unrest. Moslems had threatened the Mediterranean area. Vikings had raided from the north. After Charlemagne, the Holy Roman Empire had fallen into disorder. Many generations would pass before Norwegian pirates would be transferred into Norman peasants and the Crusades would begin to reopen the Levant.

By the thirteenth century the seas were freer, both north and south, for commerce. In continental Europe commerce, which depended largely on river traffic, had been taxed by countless feudal toll stations—sixty-two on the Rhine, seventy-seven on the Danube—which cost the merchant nearly as much as his cargo was worth. Nevertheless great fairs had remained the life of medieval trade. Sheltered by local barons and aided by the Church, international fairs did take place in Lyons, Frankfurt, and many other cities. The larger fairs lasted for six weeks and thus provided a year-round focus for international trade. The gradual removal of toll stations, the improvement of shipbuilding, and the development of fine harbors in Venice, Barcelona, Marseilles, near London, and elsewhere were all incentives for the international trader.

Once the Crusades had formed a bridge between Christian West and Moslem East, the country best situated to profit commercially was Italy. In the eleventh and twelfth centuries, Venice was a merchant's paradise. There the doge was elected by a greater council of merchants, and the resulting mercantile oligarchy pushed Venetian commerce out to the eastern Mediterranean and the Black Sea. Constantinople, for so long the light in the Dark Ages, was despoiled, and Venice took over, along with other cities of northern Italy, as the commercial capital of the world. Nowhere did this early mercantilism develop more fully than in the Tuscan city of Florence with its great wool guilds. Its powerful bankers and merchants were among the first to form a middle class strong enough to challenge the nobility.

While Italian commerce was setting the stage for the great intellectual and artistic Renaissance, an equally important commercial development was taking place in northern Europe. The German counterpart of the Italian merchant's guild was an organization called a Hansa, and to promote international cooperation and make it possible for merchants to function abroad free of pirates, highwaymen, and tax collectors, the commercial towns of northern Europe formed the Hanseatic League. There were twenty-four member cities to start with, but many more joined. For a time the league monopolized continental trade, established commercial laws, and encouraged the growth of a strong middle class of merchants, which became more than a match for the feudal barons.

Craftsman Guilds   After the establishment of merchant guilds or Hansas came the craftsman guilds. Venice alone sheltered some fifty-eight craftsman guilds, and by the thirteenth century the artisans had established collective power equal to that of the merchants, a development closely paralleled by modern labor unions in their relationship to today's capitalists. If the growth of medieval commerce brought with it primitive capitalism, it was not capitalism in the contemporary sense, but a kind of corporate town capitalism. In each town the merchants and artisans were organized by charter into guilds. Each guild was empowered to carry on a specific trade monopoly within the town itself. Regulations were strict as to employment and pricing. The number of apprentices was limited. Before work could be farmed out, an option had to be given to other guild members. Within a guild, no one member could get a monopoly on raw materials, for any surplus had to be sold at cost to fellow members. Officially, there was no competition between guild members, and if goods were inferior, meat rotten, or beer watered, an offender could be dragged through the streets with the products hung around his neck. Such enforced morality broke down, however, with reference to other towns.

The old religious rule of morality and a fair price gradually gave way to the rule of "Let the buyer beware."

Protestantism   The Roman Catholic church had been an economic beneficiary of Italy's commercial successes. In the fourteenth and fifteenth centuries, it became in large part the sponsor of the great intellectual and artistic Renaissance, which concentrated in Florence, Rome, and Venice. Even in the days of its greatest glory, however, the church was being threatened by new ideas. It had flourished in an agricultural society. Under the influence of the new commerce and the powerful merchant class, material interests began to replace spiritual concerns. By the early 1500s, the old prohibition against "usury" was being universally ignored. Monarchs were beginning to free themselves from church domination.

This onslaught from without was internalized in 1517 when a German priest, Martin Luther, attacked the papal practice of indulgences and quite unwittingly began the Protestant Reformation. Among his other accomplishments, Luther translated the Bible into German and made the individual's interpretation of the Scriptures the basis of his new Protestant faith. This approach heralded a return to the Judaic teachings of the Old Testament. Further, it advocated a frugal, hardworking life and the repudiation of lavish display. Thus a new spiritual foundation was set, sanctifying hard work and justifying the later grass-roots capitalism.

Mercantilism   Other important influences were at work during the fourteenth and fifteenth centuries. The decline of the crusading zeal witnessed a reciprocal growth of Moslem power, which proceeded to dominate the Mediterranean and threatened to absorb continental Europe. No longer had Europe direct access to eastern markets, and the search for new trade routes led to the discovery and early exploitation of the Western Hemisphere. Geographical discoveries opened up such possibilities for trade that the national state finally buried the old order based on Church and nobility. The new kingdoms needed armies to defend and enlarge their borders. Armies lived off taxes, and the fattest purses around belonged to the new merchant and banking classes. The majority of rulers found it expedient to keep these purses well filled.

In spite of disastrous wars, the growth process was complimentary and rapid. The armies protected the merchants and the merchants prospered, yielding more tax money to support bigger armies, build highways, and expand overseas trade. The pope and the feudal barons had given way to the king and his countinghouse. Mercantilism had come into its own, and the new order had its prophets. Foremost was a Florentine statesman, Machiavelli, whose book *The Prince* analyzed ways of gaining political power and establishing state supremacy over all other sources of power, including the church.

The seventeenth-century Italian city-states had few mineral resources to produce actual wealth in the sense of bullion, nor was their land the best for agriculture, but they had among their citizens a wealth of experienced artisans and merchant captains and also held a commanding position in the Mediterranean area. From trade and manufacture had come their greatness, and a Calabrian, Antonio Serra, in supplementing Machiavelli, was the first to produce a theoretical argument for the value of commerce to a nation. In *A Brief Treatise on the Causes Which Can Make Gold and Silver Plentiful in Kingdoms Where There Are No Mines,* he asserted that industry was superior to agriculture since its products could more easily be sold abroad for money, while agriculture depended on the seasons.

Undoubtedly the biggest and most successful of the crown-sponsored and chartered merchant groups was the British East India Company, which got its start in 1601 by exploiting the East Indies. In 1613 one of the company ships foundered, and it was discovered to be carrying a large amount of gold bullion out of England, an act that many regarded as draining the nation of its wealth. This could have brought the end to a promising beginning had not the son of a London merchant, Thomas Mun, come to the company's defense. It was Mun who later developed the international-balance-of-payments theory. He described the export surplus as the chief goal of national policy and urged the crown to exercise its power to aid its merchants in endeavors that would bring about such a result. The effort paid off handsomely for the East India Company, which in time exploited nearly all India, turning it into Britain's cotton field for over a hundred years until the crown took charge in the mid-nineteenth century.

In France, another statesman brought mercantilism to its full flower in the second half of the seventeenth century. Jean Baptiste Colbert, minister of finance and near dictator under Louis XIV, advanced a policy called Colbertism that granted monopolies to encourage new enterprises, especially in over-seas trade. The results were to double the king's revenues and make France the most powerful nation in Europe, with the most formidable navy. The enterprising merchants and crafts-men needed the national state as much as the state needed them. Even domestically, the crown built, maintained, and guarded highways and waterways and abolished the oppres-sive private tolls on them. But it was in overseas trade that the merchants and their king worked hand-in-glove, with the mer-chants little more than instruments of state policy to exploit other states. It was an article of faith that in each commercial transaction one party gained at the expense of the other. No one conceived then of mutual benefit. Rather, a kind of eco-nomic war existed, with the state sending forth its merchant warriors. The final objective, then as now, was a favorable bal-ance of payments. This meant more gold and silver coming into the national treasury than going out of it. In bullion there was power.

The impact of mercantilism was twofold. It encouraged the growth of national power at the expense of the nobility and the clergy, and it established both internal and international commercial markets. Since private agencies lacked sufficient resources, mercantile imperialism was at the time the only practical way to open up the New World frontier. But there were many who suffered in the process. By this time the guilds were falling into decay. They were not structured to handle new factory methods and divisions of labor, and they had be-come so exclusive that journeymen workers were forced, un-protected, into the arms of the big employers.

Mercantilism did, indeed, create vast wealth, but it fun-neled it all into the hands of merchants, financiers, manu-facturers, and their allied governments. Workers and tenant farmers felt the squeeze. Gone were the feudal rights and du-ties of the artisan. He and his peasant-farmer contemporary served primarily as instruments of production for national profit. The goal was distinct from the welfare of the population, which was encouraged to increase simply to augment the work force. As early as the Tudor period, women and children clad in rags had begun working deep in English coal mines. In Africa and South America, the opening of the new frontiers led to exploitation of the native populations, which were frequently slaughtered or enslaved. Even in North America, Britain used her colonies as a source of supply for materials lacking or more expensive in the mother country.

Antimercantilism Voices of discontent began to be heard in the late seventeenth century. In England, Dudley North, a prosperous merchant, insisted that the control of trade merely to achieve a favorable balance of payments would in the long run reduce real wealth. Later, economic liberals claimed to find the source of true wealth in neither bullion, trade, nor agriculture. As Marx would after them, they found it in human labor, for it was human effort that transformed raw material into marketable produce. The key to prosperity, therefore, was human motivation, and the incentive to work was what the government must foster. John Locke, around the end of the seventeenth century, had already described this incentive as private property. He had pointed out that the formerly great Turkish empire had withered away because the government had dictated economic policies and seized private property without justification, thus depriving the citizen of his reason for labor. Human output, the economic liberals said, not a heap of gold, was the means to national greatness, and it could only flourish in an environment of unrestricted free enterprise.

As France had been foremost in developing mercantile theories, she again took the initiative in denouncing them. A pioneer theorist was François Quesnay, who saw true wealth not in industry and trade, but in agriculture. For him, agriculture was the only source of surplus wealth, and from this source alone money flowed through the whole economy in the form of rent, payments for purchases, and wages. One of his disciples, Jacques Turgot, rose to become the French minister of finance and began to introduce antimercantilist reforms on the basis of natural economic laws. He pictured these laws functioning like the flow of blood in the human body. Followers of this school of economic naturalism became known as Physiocrats. They held that natural law worked throughout the universe, in every aspect of life, including the economy. These beliefs led to the first great principle of capitalist free enterprise, expressed as *"Laissez faire! Laissez passer!"* ("Let them do [as they wish]! Let them pass!"), thus urging an end to state monopolies and to state intrusion on the natural business process. It was time for capitalism to be unchained.

Classical Capitalism

Although eighteenth-century economists were moving away from mercantilism, the reigning monarchs of Europe remained dedicated to it. Their preoccupation with foreign trade and national power made for a century of conflict, particularly between Britain and France. A major battlefield for guns and trade goods was the North American continent. There Britain, favoring its Hudson's Bay Company, defeated France only to foster a revolution of its colonies by the continuance of its oppressive mercantile policies of taxation, exploitation, and the prohibition of settlement west of the Alleghenies. Although this stand was often justified on the grounds of consideration for the native inhabitants, "the noble savages," protecting the domain of its trading companies was the actual motivation.

While thus provoking and finally losing her American colonies, Britain was undergoing a growing industrial revolution back home that was steadily moving economic fact to fit emerging theory. The machine was breaking the direct link between agriculture and handicrafts on one side and the huge trading companies on the other. It was also introducing a new breed of individual to the world of economics. Neither royally endowed nor inherently wealthy, here was a man whose drive and ability outstripped his beginnings. With a modest investment in the new steam-powered equipment, he could employ other men to operate his machinery, thus vastly exceeding in terms of production what one artisan or a guild of workers could create with hand tools. With his capital invested in a small but growing factory, the first true capitalist had emerged.

Adam Smith   It took a Scotsman to put this confounding change into palatable perspective. Adam Smith, the founder of modern economics, was born in Kirkcaldy, Scotland, in 1723. Apart from a brief abduction by gypsies, his childhood was uneventful. He attended the University of Glasgow, then Oxford, and finally settled down quietly back at Glasgow University as a professor of moral philosophy. The work was demanding, and his thoughts might never have found their way to paper had he not been hired as the private tutor for the young duke of Buccleuch, an employment that made for three easy years in France and a pension for life on which he could live and write.

While in France, Smith discovered and absorbed the theories of the Physiocrats, and in the significant year of 1776 he published *An Inquiry into the Nature and Causes of the Wealth of Nations.* Lost in international tumult, the book had little impact on the commercial world and Smith lived out his life as no more than an absentminded philosopher, who once, clad only in a dressing gown, took a wrong turning in his garden. Deep in thought, he never realized his mistake until aroused by the church bells of Dunfermline, seventeen miles from home.

Formerly the universe had been fixed and ordained by God. Each man had a certain set place in society with privileges limited to his station in life. But this spiritually ordered universe was fading when Adam Smith pondered on his garden paths. Isaac Newton had already spoken out for a new understanding of the laws of nature in physical science. In politics, John Locke had argued that the state should serve only to support natural laws and that within this structure the individual should have free play. The new philosophical universe was composed of the unchanging machinery of nature rather than moral precepts from God. The lifting of religious restraints was in keeping with the ruthless expansion of the British Empire from Canada to India. The rule of natural law seemed to support new invention, particularly the expanding of industry; here humble origins were no barrier, and thousands of men were acting for themselves alone.

The Natural Law of Free Enterprise   What was recognized soon after his death was that in *The Wealth of Nations* Adam Smith had extended the earlier-defined natural laws of science and politics to economics. His doctrines, once accepted, drove a stake through the heart of mercantilism, which had insisted that without governmental supervision economic activity would lapse into chaos. Smith, on the other hand, was convinced that business, left to its own devices, would achieve a system responsive to natural economic laws, and hence one that worked for the mutual benefit of all. This theoretical about-face depended on three assumptions: first, that man is selfish; second, that man, if left on his own, will be the best judge of his own self-interest and maximize it, and finally, that the welfare of society is the sum of all these individual welfares.

Elaborating on his premise of self-interest, Smith saw it making for an exchange of value, with that received being more valuable to the recipient than what he gave for it. This uniform effort of each man to improve his lot would lead as though impelled by an "invisible hand" to maximizing the public good as well. As long as the natural system was not interfered with, the process was unavoidable. All government had to do for free enterprise was to maintain justice, furnish national defense, erect public works, and provide the institutions that were too complex for individuals to create. Smith did admonish businessmen not to conspire for their own advantage at public expense, but he did not envision the growth of private monopolies. This was a simpler, essentially corporation-free age, and apart from the foreign-trade monopolies, Smith scarcely imagined big business beyond the operation of a pin factory with two dozen workers employed.

With self-interest the impelling force of the economic machine, Smith envisioned a tidy mechanism of self-adjusting markets where each proffered item had a natural price based on the cost of production and adjusted to public demand. Should the quantity of a given product exceed the demand of the purchasing public, then its price must fall. Where the demand exceeded the sum of goods available, the price would rise, and, drawn by rising prices, more producers would compete for sales. Once more the supply would become excessive and prices would fall in natural harmonic rhythm. In this way the market would retain a basic self-regulating equilibrium for the greatest social good. Quite correctly, Adam Smith predicted the rapid growth of laissez-faire production and labor, with the workers' wages being happily controlled by the same rules of supply and demand that governed prices. Similar rules applied to world trade, where free markets would benefit, all through the principle of enlightened self-interest.

It made splendid sense on paper, but already the self-sufficient artisan had in large part yielded to the wage earner; and the wage earner, who might, in a small firm, bargain face to face with his boss, was giving way to the wage slave. The alternative of a healthy peasant life on the farm was quickly passing from that of reality into the realm of nostalgia. But the system seemed so simple, and irrefutably logical at the time.

However, times would continue to change and flaws would become more evident. While belief in the theory of supply and demand basically persists to this day, the idea of a freely contracting worker participating in an equitable distribution of profits fell foul of the growing power and greed of the capitalist. Overriding self-interest and unequal power would in time arouse such world-shaking reactions as those of Karl Marx and, even where revolutions were avoided or overcome, capitalism would be vastly changed. Nevertheless, two centuries of upheaval have done nothing to shake Adam Smith's position as the father of modern economics and the formulator of the theory of capitalism.

In the Western world, Smith's followers would dominate economic theory for the next one hundred years, advocating policies of business freedom and governmental restraint, free international trade and unrestricted movement of capital. Amongst them, they would refine and elaborate Smith's system while all around the real world changed. The American colonies had already broken away from their mother country. France had initiated a far bloodier revolution. Both revolutions called for individual liberty and minimal government, vital ingredients in the development of laissez-faire capitalism.

Initially, Britains had sympathized with the French Revolution. This feeling faded in the reign of terror and bloodshed that gave way finally to the seemingly endless Napoleonic wars. Industry in many nations was more than ever called upon to support this first modern war. Factories grew in size. Methods were standardized. The steam engine came of age, thereby revolutionizing transportation on land and sea, as well as providing a vital power source for other uses. Industrial cities grew up, and with them came slums.

The Malthusian Law   Industries gave power to the capitalist and gradually fettered the worker, who no longer saw his employer but took what he was offered for sixteen hours' hard labor a day. He worked without complaint, or starved. Usually he did a bit of both, and when voices of social protest began to mutter, there were economists ready with simplistic answers. One of these was Thomas Robert Malthus, who had lived his life as an obscure minister and economics teacher until he took up the moral problem of England's poor and destitute. Shorn of embroidery, his conclusion was that the only solution to poverty was more poverty, a thesis that he worked out very logically. To raise wages above the worker's subsistence level would not enhance his well-being but would only encourage him to have more children. The population would increase. Jobs would become unavailable and the workers, in increased numbers, would again know starvation. Relief for the poor led to the same result, and one can hear Scrooge on Christmas Eve denouncing charity and the surplus population. This do-nothing solution was certainly a solace to the capitalists who felt themselves urged on to greater production in the pious hope that it might outstrip the growing legions of the poor and thus indirectly improve their lot.

This basic doctrine was accepted by David Ricardo, the son of a Dutch Jewish immigrant to England, who became the apostle of capital accumulation. Given the Malthusian law of population, hope for the future lay in capital investment and rapid growth of business, the only true form of economic progress. Ricardo wrote at a time when hard-pressed farmers were clamoring for protective grain tariffs, a device against which he argued strenuously. As he saw it, the tariff would raise food costs, thereby necessitating a raise in workers' wages, all to the detriment of business profit and recapitalization. Thanks in large part to Malthus and Ricardo, the farmer was to know much of the hardship already experienced by his industrial-worker cousin.

Enlarging on his theory of unrestrictive world markets, Ricardo said that trade policies designed to protect domestic producers would only bring injury to the nation as a whole. By way of example, he pointed out that if Britain's industrial mills could produce, per man-hours of work, cloth worth in France twice what the same man-hours could produce in wheat, it would pay Britain to shift her economic efforts from wheat to cloth. Then one day's worth of cloth could be exchanged for two days' worth of wheat and all would be better off. The formula could be enlarged to show how even France, lacking Britain's mills, would profit from the arrangement.

Once again it looked very convincing on paper despite a general depression following the Napoleonic war boom, a depression that lasted for thirty years. Needless to say, this prolonged slump brought criticism and unrest, revolutions in Europe, a near revolution in Britain, and Karl Marx, whose anticapitalist mania sowed the seeds of future upheaval.

Say's Law of Markets   An early response to criticism came from a Frenchman, Jean Baptiste Say. He extended Adam Smith's ideas into a Law of Markets that retained vitality until the Great Depression of the 1930s. Say's Law of Markets asserted that the production of any item is met by an equivalent demand. Brief shortages might occur in one place, surpluses in another, but over the long haul these minor difficulties are resolved by industry adjusting its production. Thus an economic depression was simply the result of misdirected production and would always be solved in time by the naturally self-interested forces within industry.

Jeremy Bentham, whose skeleton topped by a wax head still attends board meetings at the University of London, was left to round out the picture. Concerned more with sociology and ethics than with large economic schemes, Bentham nevertheless worked out what he called a "hedonistic calculus" for each individual. This scheme identified a human being's day-by-day behavior of seeking pleasure and avoiding pain with the same mechanical law that the laissez-faire economists saw applying to world economics and the scientists attached with more justice to the universe. In this way, the mechanical picture was complete. From the natural laws that dictated international trade right down to the pleasure-pain decisions of the poorest individual, all human conduct responded to the principle of enlightened self-interest.

Last of the classic school of economists was John Stuart Mill, who died in 1873. Mill did not deny the traditional economic laws, but as a humanitarian, he could not accept the inevitability of industrial evils and their toll in human suffering. He sought a midpoint between laissez-faire and social reform. For favoring the ownership of factories by workers, he was called a socialist. For suggesting a minor, nonprogressive income tax, he was called insane. Like Adam Smith, Mill lived and died before his time.

The Birth of
American Capitalism

By her mercantile policies, Britain had consistently discouraged industry and hence incipient capitalism in the American colonies, but in so doing she had encouraged a thirst for independence and freedom of all sorts, not the least of which was economic. The American Revolution, which might have impoverished a more developed land, actually encouraged expansion, for the penniless government paid off its debts by land grants to its veterans. New land was boundless and cheap. The move west was on before the last shot was fired.

The United States Constitution, which has been for so long hallowed and, despite protestations, so much altered in interpretation, was framed by prosperous men concerned with securing their own property against the future state's legislative power to confiscate or tax. The thoughts of John Locke and Adam Smith moved the pens of the Founding Fathers to write of the God-given right of life, liberty, and the pursuit of happiness, and the natural and inalienable right to property. Such rights existed beyond man's power to alter them, and the state was merely a device to protect such rights, never to create, diminish, or redefine them. About the only flaw any of the signers saw in this idyllic scene made up of independent small farmers and local merchants was the fact that among available property were human beings. However, even in the South, slavery seemed to be dying a natural death, and a war had to be won. Cotton had not yet become king.

American Individualism   So the United States got off to a running start, full of frontier individualism and the conviction that a man has the right to his own property and can do with it as he pleases. Real estate was the first American growth industry, an expansion begun with the successful conclusion of the revolution and augmented by the more dubious results of the War of 1812. During this period, the United States remained true to its early dream, a nation of small farmers, receptive to the Jeffersonian notion that the federal economic function should be nil. After all, if life in the growing eastern cities began to be oppressive, a man could always pack up his family and head west.

Along with the judgment that the individual was a better protector of his own property interests than the state went a ready acceptance of the corporation form. The corporation had originally been regarded as a privileged type of organization reserved for the performance of public services such as turnpike- and bridge-building. Now it became readily available to the individual for his own business purposes, carrying with it the distinct advantages of limited liability for stockholders and business continuity uninterrupted by death. Thus, unknowingly, a future age of industrial giants was conceived.

Capitalism had not gotten very far in the United States and the potentials of incorporation had scarcely been explored when the United States became involved in another unpopular war. This was in the mid-1840s, with Mexico. The causes were imperialistic, but agrarian rather than capitalistic. Only the rural South was in favor of the war, for the results promised to extend her cotton fields westward. This expansion of the cotton business would tend to boost the price of slaves upon which the Southern economy depended. Curiously, although the war was resisted in the North, it was the North that truly prospered, with an industrial boom, cheaply fed by Irish labor fleeing the potato famine in Ireland.

While in the United States capitalism was flexing its first real muscles and wagon trains rolled westward toward the endless horizon and the golden dream, Europe, which had no dream of empty spaces, was in the throes of social upheaval. In Britain, these were the "hungry forties." Charles Dickens was outlining *Hard Times* and as the decade came to a close Karl Marx arrived with the *Communist Manifesto* in which he attacked as a fraud the traditional wage bargain between worker and capitalist and presented the only alternative he saw, class war to the death.

Marx's disciples were among the immigrants flooding to the promised land, but their doctrine made little or no impression there. Wealth in America was still essentially based on land ownership. There was room for small shops and hardworking artisans. A puritan past and the admonitions of Benjamin Franklin had not yet been forgotten, and a man of industry and frugality could still go far on his own. Take John Jacob Astor, the penniless German butcher's son, who had built up the great American Fur Company, which dared to lock horns in the West with the Hudson's Bay Company. Then there was Cornelius Vanderbilt, who had taken the helm of a side-wheeler and slugged through the fever swamps of Nicaragua to compete with the Collins Line. Vanderbilt's income was $100,000 a month, gained with a ferocity that would have disturbed Franklin. Vanderbilt never bothered to take a rival to court. If need be, and with fair warning, he simply ruined them.

It took pluck and hard work to rise from poverty and become a Vanderbilt or an Astor. The early tycoon was generally admired, even if he was not beloved. Of the latter breed was "Uncle Dan" Drew, the "Great Bear" of Wall Street. He was a prune-faced man who walked like a cat dressed up in parson's clothing. Some thought he was the reincarnation of William Kidd the pirate, returned to his old Wall Street haunts. Old Uncle Dan had begun as a cattle drover, and as such he has been credited with the invention of watered stock. The night before a sale, he would feed his herd salt until the beasts were so crazed with thirst they would put on fifty pounds or more in pure water weight before the sale. Another trick attributed to the Great Bear was that of writing an order to buy massive amounts of a certain stock in the presence of avaricious colleagues. Then, while wiping his face with his handkerchief, he would conspicuously lose the note. As soon as he had wandered off, the note would be examined and acted upon by his rivals. They should have known better. Dan Drew wasn't a careless man and he would profit from their purchases. He trusted no one, not even himself, and he never put real accounts down on paper, much less inside information regarding the stock market.

The Civil War Such men were folk heroes before the Civil War. Some still are. It would take that war and another generation to fill out the image and fix it with a new title, half-admiring, half-resentful: "Robber Baron." Although the causes of the Civil War were many and some of them idealistic, economics was a prime factor. On the one hand, the Southern agricultural states resented what seemed to them to be the unconstitutional establishment of protective tariffs for the sole benefit of Northern industry. They feared, too, what seemed a growing reassessment of and threat to their basic property rights, namely the institution of chattel slavery upon which Southern solvency depended. Four years of civil war ruined the South financially and changed, seemingly forever, the basic idea of property. No longer would the national majority support and honor the property claims of slave owners. The war established once and for all that human beings cannot be bought and sold. Over one hundred years later, another injustice is being corrected, this time through the courts: the injustice of discrimination on the basis of race. This process also is altering the concept of rights in physical property and limiting them further, as with the restaurant owner who may no longer select his customers according to the color of their skin.

While the Civil War bankrupted the defeated South, it was another great boost for Northern industry, which, more than any other factor, had won the war. Particularly, it was a victory for the iron horse, which during the hostilities had been converted from wood- to coal-burning, a change more drastic and important at the time than the shift during World War II from propeller to jet-driven aircraft. Expansion burst beyond the railroad and industry. Each of the nation's wars had brought a farm boom, and the Civil War was no exception. In fact, the Northern agricultural buildup helped to finance the war by way of an increase of produce exported to England.

Peace brought a period of brief but exuberant optimism and vigorous expansion. The real winning of the West had begun without the class rancor that beset European society. There was virtually no sense of class. The land was still dominated by small farms, small towns, and businesses where the boss and a few workers toiled in close association, eating from the same table. A steel plant with over one hundred workers was considered gigantic. As long as cheap land was available, as long as pay envelopes thickened and the homestead law provided almost free admission to the bounty of the golden West, any distinction of class was avoided as a barrier to the envisioned future, which knew no bounds.

True, there was poverty. There was the shattered South, with its Negroes thrown on the labor market without land, skills, or assets. Lest this breakdown be taken as a failure of

The Birth of American Capitalism 29

the system, there were the usual intellectuals with an explanation for the existing poverty. In England Herbert Spencer had begun to turn Darwinism into a social philosophy. In society, as in nature, according to this theory, the weak were weeded out and the fittest survived. Thus the less vigorous social institutions as well as the less gifted humans perished in the struggle. This convenient message fell on listening ears in the United States, where Spencer's foremost advocate was a Yale University economist and former Episcopalian minister, William Graham Sumner. Poverty and corruption, laziness and ignorance could be eliminated only by centuries of evolution. Inexorably, society moved toward eventual perfection according to fixed laws of nature akin to the laws of the physical universe. To tamper with free competition, to hand out charity to the unfit, was to mar the operation of the machinery that God, in eons past, had set spinning. In this way Adam Smith's universe was infused with the law of the jungle. The time was ripe for the robber barons to come of age, and they were ready with tooth and claw.

The Robber Barons While in Bismarck's Germany the welfare state was being developed, in the United States rugged individualism was the order of the day. Cornelius Vanderbilt was admonishing his enemies, "What do I care about the law? Ain't I got the power?" "Big Jim" Fisk could casually comment, after the criminal misuse of other people's money, that nothing was lost save honor, and honor to Big Jim clearly had little market value. Most of these early robber barons (some called them more politely "the Florentines of the North") came from the northeast, bringing an insatiable money lust masked by an air of puritan piety. In dark moments of financial crisis, Daniel Drew sought out the Lord. John D. Rockefeller, as a boy, had passed the plate in church. As a man, he would teach Bible class, confident throughout life that his success was a reward from God.

Many churchmen believed it, too, or so one would gather from their sermons, which went to great lengths to defend the growing business trusts as sound Christian institutions. No wonder, when J. P. Morgan could be counted on for half a million dollars to erect the Cathedral of Saint John the Divine in New York City. One could commend the widow's mite, but it was the robber barons' gold that built churches. Not all such money was sanctified on the altar. The barons knew how to spend as well as make dollars; or if they did not, their sons did. There were often lavish parties at Delmonico's, where, to surprise the guests, oyster cocktails would be seeded with black pearls, or every lady might find wrapped in her napkin a gold bracelet bearing her host's initials. One baron's son saw fit to enhance his smile by having his teeth set with diamonds.

The most unscrupulous tycoon of this conscienceless age was Jay Gould. Like many of his fellows, he began in poverty, the frail, stunted, cow-minding son of a poor farmer. In school he gained some attention with a composition entitled "Honesty Is the Best Policy." Perhaps he still held this Franklinesque faith when he arrived in New York City with a better mousetrap. The trap, with which he planned to make his fortune, was promptly stolen. One might assume a rapid change of conviction on young Gould's part except for the fact that the trap was retrieved and in the end gave him a start. From mousetraps he progressed to a managerial post in a leather-goods company. So thoroughly did Gould manipulate the company books that the owner felt obliged to commit suicide. No pause for moral reflection here; when the heirs took over the tannery, Gould attacked and captured the building with a drunken squad of hired toughs.

By this time the maturing Gould was launched on his ceaseless quest for economic power, an undertaking undeterred by sentiment, conscience, patriotism, justice, piety, pity, or the desire for admiration. He had agents but no friends, and numerous enemies who were held physically at bay by plainclothes police. When defeat finally came, it would not be at his enemies' hands. It would come from within, and was known in those days as "consumption," which he dared not disclose lest the financial hounds set upon his blood trail.

Gould had no joy of money, no sensuous side, but he had a dream of power. From childhood he longed to build a transcontinental railroad. His first big operation involved the Erie Railroad. Through manipulation of its stock, he and others, including Jim Fisk, managed to milk it of some $9 million. As a result of this adventure and still in combination with Fisk, Gould tried, in 1869, to corner the free gold supply in New York's money market. Before the deal was completed, President Grant's brother-in-law had been brought into the scheme, to tie the hands of the federal government, and the price of gold had been driven sky-high. The federal government acted only after these men had sold out at a gigantic profit, thereby causing a financial panic.

Not until the 1870s did Gould's financial talents fully mature, and then, in his own warped way, he turned them upon his childhood dream. The first step, no minor one, was to gain a controlling interest in the Union Pacific Railroad, which spanned the country. Once in the saddle, Gould was not content to build up a great transportation empire. Paralleling the bright tracks of the Union Pacific across the nation were the rusty streaks of the moribund Kansas Pacific and Denver Pacific lines. No rivalry, in fact, existed, but Gould bought up the Kansas and Denver lines with the idea of forcing the Union Pacific to purchase them at favorable terms. While his fellow directors of the Union Pacific resisted purchase of this worthless combination, Gould circulated exaggerated reports of their rejuvenation (he had the advantage of owning several newspapers). In the end the Union Pacific was forced to buy the lines at a net profit to Gould of $10 million, with virtually no actual benefit to the railroad itself.

Gould's adventures seldom served the public interest. His

last major undertaking was similar and typical. It involved the New York elevated train system. Gould began by attacking the system through his newspapers until the stock fell dangerously. Then he bought it up, and the newspapers began to discover that the elevated train company was solvent after all. Needless to say, this and his other manipulations enlisted a host of enemies. As his health declined, they marshaled their forces. In a typical scheme, when the wires of his telegraph line were blown down by a storm, they planted a messenger boy to deliver to them Gould's secret communications. By 1884, they had him on the run. Gould fought back in a novel way. He threatened them privately that he would declare public bankruptcy, an occurrence so vast as to panic the financial world. They relented. Gould continued to fight back until his death in 1892, when he still had the gall to describe his most nefarious stock dealings as responsive to the public demand of widows and orphans.

If Jay Gould was the least civic-minded of the robber barons, he was not the biggest. Since the 1830s, the oil of Titusville, Pennsylvania, had been used for patent medicine. After twenty years it began to rival whale oil as an illuminant. By the 1860s, the oil fields of Pennsylvania and Ohio were a confusion of hand-hewn derricks and shacks constantly ravaged by fires and other disasters that kept the price of oil shifting and the supply uncertain. This was the situation when John D. Rockefeller went into the refining business. He began as one refiner among dozens, but, like Gould, he had a purpose, and neither conscience, friends, nor diversions to stand in its way. With a record of dependability that exceeded his competitors, Rockefeller was able to work a secret deal with a number of carriers, including the New York Central Railroad, whereby, for a guaranteed amount of cargo, he would be returned a rebate, or refund, on the standard carrying fee. The effect was cumulative. Rockefeller sold for less and began to sell more. The railroads became increasingly dependent on his growing business. Competitors were absorbed. In 1870, Rockefeller incorporated as the Standard Oil Company of Ohio.

He was just beginning. Two years earlier, the Michigan Salt Association had been formed to overcome a confused market situation over the sale of salt from the area. Stability and price-fixing were the result, and Rockefeller duly noted the possibilities of a similar approach for the Pennsylvania oil fields, where small-scale competition among refiners was cutthroat and wasteful. His tactic was the old secret freight rebate. This, coupled with a process of combining with a few major operators while driving the rest out of business, led to formation of the South Improvement Company. Rivals fell like dominoes, bought up or ruined by price-fixing. Within a space of three months, twenty-five competitors vanished from the scene, and the Standard Oil Company of Ohio had a virtual monopoly.

What John D. Rockefeller was to the business monopoly, J. P. Morgan was to finance. His first notable success was the purchase of defective rifles from the government during the Civil War. These were purchased cheaply, then sold back to another federal agency at a huge markup. This was not J.P.'s only questionable contribution to the war effort. What Morgan understood best was money, and at this time most of it was in London. Money meant gold, and as Morgan correctly anticipated, a great deal would be required to support the federal government during the Civil War. With this in mind, he rounded up all the available gold he could find in the United States. Half of it he shipped off to storage in London, thereby driving up the price of what gold remained in the country. This was a cake that Morgan had and ate at the same time, for British companies were planning to build ships for the confederacy, and Washington needed a large amount of ready gold to make Britain breach the contract. At a considerable profit, Morgan made his London hoard available to the government.

During the war Jay Cooke had financed the United States

treasury. In the early 1870s, Morgan muscled in on this monopoly, and by 1873 he had the pleasure of pushing Cooke under. The resulting panic, depression, and general public distress was treated by Morgan as nothing but mass incompetency. When a number of years later President Cleveland approached Morgan about a meeting with the secretary of the treasury, Morgan had the arrogance to remark, "Send your man to see my man."

The great capitalists were not all criminal or soulless men. Though historian Charles Francis Adams, Jr., would sum them up as "a set of mere money-getters and traders, essentially unattractive and uninteresting," his statement is suspect, as he himself was ousted from the presidency of the Union Pacific by Jay Gould. They were not all Jay Goulds. John D. Rockefeller, before he died when he was nearly one hundred years old, would give away over half a billion dollars.

Andrew Carnegie, born to poor weavers in Scotland, was brought to the United States at the age of thirteen and first went to work as a bobbin-boy in a cloth mill in Allegheny, Pennsylvania. Eventually he would be nicknamed the "white-haired Scotch devil," but before he died he donated money to build the Peace Palace at The Hague that now houses the International Court of Justice, not to mention endowing American libraries and educational institutions.

Best beloved of these captains of industry was hulking, lantern-jawed Peter Cooper, inventor and ironmaster, whose success began with a run-down glue factory and some Manhattan real estate. At a time when others believed in power, not law, and supported old Dan Drew's motto, "It's the still hog that eats the most," Cooper had the perverse notion that vast fortunes should be held as a sort of social trust. Without the inducement of tax relief that encourages today's philanthropists, Peter Cooper, after spending his youth making money, devoted his maturity to giving it away. This freak among the robber barons ran for the presidency at the age of eighty-five on the Greenback platform devoted to a program of saving farmers and laborers from hopeless debt. He was a pioneer supporter of a program of compulsory education, but his most lasting success was Cooper Union for the Advancement of Science and Art. This New York City institution, which is still going strong, has provided free courses in a range of subjects—chemistry, physics, music, art—for gifted but impoverished students. Peter Cooper may have been eccentric. Indeed, some thought him daft, but he was a conscience to the Carnegies and the Rockefellers, and he set the pattern of philanthropy that has mellowed the image of the robber barons. When Peter Cooper died, the city of New York wept, and thousands formed up behind his hearse.

The last quarter of the nineteenth century seldom experienced such unified sentiment. Feelings regarding big business were rapidly polarizing. The exuberant postwar boom ended with the panic of 1873, which ushered in hard times. Only a few industrial giants prospered by gobbling up their less hearty fellows. It was a year, too, made memorable by the famous Slaughterhouse Cases. They involved a Louisiana law for the benefit of public health that limited the operation of slaughterhouses and virtually created a monopoly. Independent butchers and cattle dealers were against this restriction of free enterprise, but the Supreme Court held that it was a valid exercise of the police power.

This unprecedented decision was followed three years later by *Munn* v. *Illinois,* in which operators of grain elevators questioned the right of the state to set a maximum charge for storing and handling grain. The operators said the state was confiscating their assets without due process, but the Supreme Court again strengthened the role of state government by calling the action "regulation," and not "deprivation."

Reform from the top seemed to be on the move. Then came the great Haymarket Square riots in Chicago. Higher prices, wage reductions, and layoffs led to this violence, which

36   C A P I T A L I S M culminated in the death by bombing of several policemen, and the seizure and execution of alleged anarchists.

The establishment was frightened and the Supreme Court stepped back from decisions in support of the seemingly ungrateful "little man." In the Slaughterhouse Cases, Justice Stephen J. Field had dissented from the majority opinion on the grounds that such governmental intervention was like stealing a God-given right. By the mid 1880s, the rest of the Supreme Court had come around to his view, and much supervisory state legislation, such as child-labor laws, was struck down in favor of unrestrained laissez-faire. The myth of Ragged Dick and Tattered Tom, both characters of popular fiction, rising from the immigrant slums to become tycoons and finally beloved elder statesmen was refurbished. Capitalists could point with pride to old Andrew Carnegie, who had begun at twenty cents a day; yet somehow his twenty million a year seemed unconscionably greater than the $600 per annum he was paying his steel workers.

The result was an ambivalent feeling of sympathy and fear toward the deprived worker. Rather like a large and penned-up dog, there was doubt whether, upon his release, he would lick one's hand from gratitude or bite it off. The consensus seemed to favor letting sleeping dogs lie. To bolster this position intellectually and as a counter to Marxian doctrine came the neoclassical economists. Unhappily for classical economic theorists, Marx had taken their theory of the value of labor and turned it into his own idea of exploitation. Undeniably the development of machinery had done much to outmode the old labor theory, and the neoclassicists abandoned it for the dubious principle of marginal utility.

The Theory of Marginal Utility This theory held that the value of a product or service depended not on the embodied labor but upon the usefulness of the last unit purchased. Relying on Bentham's mathematics of pleasure versus pain, the idea was that the consumer, faced with alternatives for spending his income, will seek to maximize his satisfaction. In simplest terms, the assumption behind this theory is that a purchaser will pay less the more he obtains of a desired object. If a man is starving, he will pay an exorbitant price for a loaf of bread. As his stomach fills, a second loaf becomes less attractive, and he will presumably continue paying the demanded price only as long as the bread gives him more pleasure than the pain involved in parting with his money. The last loaf purchased, called the marginal loaf, sets the limit on his demand. Since in practice a day's supply of bread would be purchased at one time, not one portion at a time at diminishing prices, the price of the marginal loaf establishes the price of the entire batch. In this way prices and values under the new theory would adjust in the same old way, but for a refurbished reason that sidestepped Marx and gave renewed support to laissez-faire free enterprise.

So the big three, Carnegie, Morgan, and Rockefeller ("Reckafellow," as some called him) rolled right along to bigger and better things. In the 1890s, Carnegie was selling armor plate to Russia, and he controlled 70 percent of all steel exports. The other two capitalists were worth so much that they could flood the market with securities at their pleasure and, when the market fell under the weight of selling, take it all back at their leisure. The big monopolies had arrived, and ever since *Darcy* v. *Allein* in 1602 any sort of monopoly had been held suspect. In this old English case, a monopoly granted by Queen Elizabeth I to a certain manufacturer of playing cards had been invalidated by the court, which held the monopoly was against public interest as it deprived men of work while encouraging high prices and reducing quality. In 1624, the Statute of Monopolies invalidated all crown-granted monopolies except those for inventors' patents.

In the United States, the first such legislation arrived in 1890 with the Sherman Antitrust Act. The objective of this law was to protect society from exploitation and from the taking of unfair advantage for profit's sake, by ensuring free competition. This goal was beneficial both to the consuming public and to the small businessman who was endangered by large price wars. More narrowly, the terms of the act held contracts in restraint of trade or commerce to be illegal, thus making an equation between conspiracy and monopoly. The effect was to make the big firms bigger simply because the older agreements that might be regarded as in restraint of trade were replaced by actual mergers.

Business went on as usual. The Supreme Court had little respect for the Sherman Act and believed that government at most should be a policeman, avoiding if possible any business tax and rarely invoking the antitrust law. Poverty, when it occurred, was an individual matter, indicating a defect in character rather than a social problem. Yet a clamor from the lower depths was rising, and not the least of the voices raised on behalf of the poor belonged to Pope Leo XIII. In his encyclical *Rerum novarum,* he called for justice animated by charity, for a return to community values, and for a kind of welfare society, with work hours limited, minimum wages set, and an end to child labor. But was it fair to prevent an ambitious boy of ten or eleven from getting ahead in life by working sixteen hours a day in a coal mine? Opinions were divided.

Revamping American Capitalism

In the United States, pressure that would lead to explosion or reform began building after the Civil War. It reached the headlines on a morning in 1873, when a newsboy, loudly announcing the failure of Jay Cooke's bank, was arrested for spreading false rumors. The news, however, was all too true. Hard times had hit business and industry. They had not neglected the farmer, either, for whom the rosy western glow had darkened. Many were returning to the East, their creaking wagons emblazoned with such slogans as "In God we trusted, in Kansas we busted." The country swarmed with train robbers and tramps, normally farmhands and workers who drifted now in dangerous gangs. Jesse James became a living legend. Bitter strikes broke out when a railroad decreed a 10 percent wage cut without decreasing high dividends on watered stock. In Pittsburgh, where the pro-business government sent troops against the railroad workers, twenty-five people were killed before the troops retired to a roundhouse, which the mob duly fired with cars full of burning coke. Stores and railroad cars were looted and, before exhaustion brought a return to order, a grain elevator, 2 roundhouses, and 125 locomotives were destroyed.

This first outburst of discontent inspired less sympathy than fear and resistance. The government stuck by its monopoly makers. Abraham Lincoln's son was up to his ears in building utility trusts. The old close relationship between owner and worker had been usurped by sheer bigness and the gulf that yawned between them was as wide as that between noble and serf. About the only organization to show real concern for the plight of the children of the poor was New York's Society for the Prevention of Cruelty to Animals.

Populism Unions, of course, were being formed, and they fought. Terence Powderley headed over half a million Knights of Labor. By the mid-eighties, they were strong enough to bring Jay Gould to the strike-settlement table, but the real hope lay in politics. In 1892, 1,300 delegates representing the deprived and downtrodden headed along dusty roads in bounding buckboards to launch, with all the confidence of Don Quixote, an attack on the economic windmills of America. These were the Populists, and they sang to the tune of the "Battle Hymn of the Republic":

> They have stolen our money, have ravished our homes;
> With the plunder erected to Mammon a throne;
> They have fashioned a god, like the Hebrews of old,
> Then bid us bow down to their image of gold.

Populism was an awkward union of midwestern farmers and urban laborers, the "producers," as they saw themselves, who worked with their hands and produced actual wealth. Though not revolutionaries, they had little use for the providers of capital, and they regarded as prime villains the owners of railroads. Against them the Populists advocated drastic government takeover. This socialistic approach extended to the telephone and telegraph systems, which were nearing monopoly and were run with disregard for the consumer's rights.

Reform Darwinism   In the election of 1892, Populism became the first third party to carry a state since 1856. Hard times continued to swell the party ranks. Militant strikes increased, and victory seemed to be at hand. A few theologians and philosophers were beginning to develop ideas favorable to Populist belief. In England, John Ruskin was writing of Christianizing the environment, and Richard Ely, after studies in Germany's welfare state, began work on a new economics, a kind of reform Darwinism based on improving the environment rather than simply accepting the harsh doctrine of survival of the fittest. Wholeheartedly Ely gave his support to organized labor while decrying the evils of capitalism.

A popularizer of Ely's ideas, and a strong advocate of reform himself, was the American economist Henry George. Raised on the notion that hard work led to success, George, from his early teens, had worked as a salesman, editor, seaman, and prospector. He remained poor from start to finish, and during the depression of the seventies he put his complaints on paper. He told about the opening of rich mines, the driving out of the Indians, the slaughter of the buffalo, the laying of rails across the West; all the new knowledge and invention that had left the mass of citizens as badly off as ever. George became a celebrity. The attraction of his book *Progress and Poverty,* published in 1879, was that it attacked conservative Darwinism with its own weapons while claiming that reform Darwinism was more scientific, with a closer relationship to the environment. Basically, George's theme disclaimed the older notion that trust magnates or street Arabs were all a result of immutable hereditary traits: that is, of the constitutional fitness to survive. His interest was in the social environment, which he felt might be improved by legislation. One need not wait for centuries to weed out the unfit genes. One could work to improve the world, and quickly.

Reform Darwinism may have been a match for older theory, but Populism at best had a sandy foundation. No coalition of poor southern whites and blacks could last long, and almost as ill-matched were the foreign-born city laborers with socialistic ideas and the midwestern farmers who would go along only so far with government ownership. But in 1896 they had a candidate for President, one they shared with the Democrats. This was William Jennings Bryan, the silver-throated orator of the corn belt. He lost the election by a narrow margin in the popular vote.

Had circumstances remained the same, results might have been very different by the turn of the century. But circumstances seldom stay the same, and by 1898 Bryan was mounted on a black horse, employing his pulpit voice to lead a regiment of cornhusker volunteers in the Spanish-American War. The voice of reform was drowning in a medley of trumpets and drums. The country went to war with a will. President McKinley went reluctantly, remarking at last with Victorian pomposity, "There was nothing left for us to do but to take them all, and to educate the Filipinos, and uplift and civilize and Christianize them, and by God's grace do the very best we could by them as our fellow-men for whom Christ also died." The prayer made, McKinley is reported to have slept well, and the Spanish-American War, in a clinical sense, was a model war, fought and won conclusively on foreign soil with little cost and much profit. What's more, it proved a shot in the arm for the economy, and capitalism moved along toward higher stages.

The Coal Strike of 1902 Reform wasn't dead, simply outshouted, but not for long. By 1900, Pennsylvania's anthracite coalfields were in decay. There, work began at the age of ten for fledgling miners, some so small their lunch buckets dragged on the ground as they proceeded at dawn to the breaker to sort slate from coal for thirty-five cents a day. During a miner's years below he would first work for others, a digger in the dangerous dark at about $1 a day. An outstanding miner might eventually employ his own gang and enter into a contract with an operator to produce coal at so much per carload. As a contractor, he might gross nearly $1,000 a year, but out of this had to come salaries for his laborers, tools, fuses, and powder, all at inflated company prices.

In a typical year, 441 miners were killed from rock falls, explosions, and the seeping in of poisonous gasses. Many more were maimed, while work grew erratic owing to fluctuation in coal prices. Unrest spread in the mining areas, and attempts to organize the miners were broken up by "coalies," the coal and iron police employed by the operators. It took a brilliant young self-educated leader, John Mitchell, who had worked below since the age of twelve, to enlarge the United Mine Workers into a formidable union. They were strong enough to strike in 1900. McKinley, running for President again on a full-dinner-pail platform, impressed the operators with the need to settle. On October 29, the workers went back to the mines on what has since been called "Mitchell Day"—a holiday throughout the anthracite country—although little had been promised and less given. A phony peace persisted throughout 1901.

The following year, in behalf of the United Mine Workers, Mitchell demanded an eight-hour day, a 20 percent wage increase, a minimum wage, and recognition of the union. The operators forecast bankruptcy and would not budge. On May 12, 147,000 workers failed to report to work, and the great anthracite strike was on. By July, the National Guard was called into the Shenandoah Valley to break up brutal fights between the strikers and the "scabs" who continued to work because their families were starving. By August, the strike was running out of gas. Morale was down. The union purse was dwindling.

The strike might have failed but for a very small spark that set off a nationwide fire of resentment. When William F. Clark, a concerned citizen, wrote a letter to George Baer, president of the Reading Coal Company, asking him to settle, Baer made the mistake of writing back, in part as follows:

> The rights and interests of the laboring man will be protected and cared for, not by the labor agitators, but by the Christian men of property to whom God has given control of the property rights of this country, and upon the successful management of which so much depends. Do not be discouraged. Pray earnestly that right may triumph, always remembering that Lord God Omnipotent still reigns, and that His reign is one of law and order, and not of violence and crime.

This classic of naïve arrogance found its way into the newspapers and was sufficient to put the public for the first time on labor's side. Also, there were other pressures. The price of coal had risen from $6 to $20 a ton. Fuel riots were expected to take place in New York, where the nights were growing longer and colder, and the Republican party was expected to pay the consequences at the upcoming congressional elections. Then President Theodore Roosevelt, recently sworn in after McKinley's assassination, called a conference. He arrived in a wheelchair, having been injured not long before in a traffic accident.

Perhaps George Baer thought him a complete cripple, for he remained blind and abusive, calling on the President to squelch the outlaws and anarchists. Baer was belaboring the wrong man. But for his official position, Roosevelt indicated, he would have thrown Baer through the window. On the other hand, Mitchell, who represented the mine workers, entirely acquiesced in the appointment of a presidential panel and promised to abide by its results. Roosevelt was favorably impressed. With the aid of J. P. Morgan, Baer was finally brought, grumbling, to arbitration, a process that took three months. Clarence Darrow represented the union. The witnesses who appeared for the miners—the blinded, the widowed, the impoverished—numbered 558, while Baer, speaking for the operators, relied on quotations from Roman law and from Seneca. The result was a compromise, a 10 percent wage increase plus other benefits. A key demand, recognition of the union, was not realized, but more vital was the gathering sympathy on the part of the public and the fact that the strike had been carried through to litigation.

Pressure for reform was not limited to the lower classes. Expansion had outlived its exuberant youth and certain self-evident facts had laid to rest the old dreams. Over a third of American farmers no longer worked their own farms. Few men still hoped to start from scratch and end up owning their own factories in a land where 1 percent of the population owned more than all the rest put together. J. P. Morgan and Andrew Carnegie had just assembled the first billion-dollar trust, and Morgan and Rockefeller controlled 341 directorships in 112 corporations. Factories, not to mention the men who labored in them, were becoming chips on the gambling table of high finance.

Thorstein Veblen Many saw the situation and were disturbed, but none spoke out with more bitter invective than the son of a Norwegian immigrant, Thorstein Veblen. Sloppy and hostile, Veblen wore a cap and Vandyke beard. His views were too radical for the colleges where he taught. Not that he cared. To encourage small classes, he lectured in a mumble and never gave a grade over C. Still, his students loved him, but his behavior held him back academically and left him teaching, as he put it, in a "rotten stump called Missouri." Though as bitter as their author, his books were an immediate success, beginning in 1899 with *The Theory of the Leisure Class*. Here Veblen saw the social standards of Western capitalism as no different behind their facade than those of Attila the Hun. Veblen despised the rich. He characterized their life-style as conspicuous waste and consumption, meaning that they did nothing but show off their wealth by bejeweling their wives, buying fine clothes in which no manual labor could be performed, and throwing expensive parties.

Five years later Veblen followed up with *The Theory of Business Enterprise,* which paid due respect to the "captains of industry" (his phrase). In them, he saw not devotion to the utility of the product, but rather a money-squeezing desire for profit that led to monopolistic and harmful control of output. Throughout his life, Veblen remained a gadfly to entrenched capitalism, and he had the satisfaction of living until 1929, when the rich and the powerful whom he so despised began their seemingly fatal slide into chaos.

With the turn of the century, fading populism had begun giving way to a more urban progressivism that looked to en-lighten business interests rather than to flatten them. Teddy Roosevelt was emerging as a patrician reformer. He was con-temptuous of the unlettered tycoon, whom he regarded as being in need of an education and sound chastisement, though he remained suspicious of the rock-throwing radicals. As the President set about his fatherly task, *McClure's Magazine,* fol-lowed by others, began a long series of articles designed to expose corruption in politics and big business. "Tweed Days in St. Louis" began the attack, and very little honor remained in high places by the time writers Ida Tarbell, Lincoln Steffens, and many others grew weary of muckraking.

The New Nationalism Roosevelt had already left to mas-ter the "mighty and terrible lords" of the African jungle when a book that would inspire his response to capitalism and re-form was published. This was *The Promise of American Life,* by Herbert Croly, a journalist and political philosopher. Roose-velt read it with the hides of lions, elephants, and rhinoceroses heaped about him. Roosevelt and Croly together made for something different: a new nationalism. In essence, Croly did not see business kept in harness by sweeping federal powers designed to represent the interest of the nation as a whole. Rather than the selfish conflict of a number of special-interest minorities, he imagined a joint movement of the entire country led by powerful officials.

Croly put his finger on a fundamental weakness in progressivism, which depended so heavily on reform Darwinism. By its emphasis on the environment, it left a built-in excuse for failure and crime. Eat, drink, and hold up the village bank. It's all the fault of the environment. Croly yearned instead for a guided "national socialism" that would encourage huge combinations of labor and capital to serve the social interests as set forth by the state. Here, too, was a basic flaw that would not become evident until the 1920s, with the rise of fascism, but it was not recognized as a problem at that time. The theory had many answers for the helpless relativism of reform Darwinism, as well as for the economic tyranny of a laissez-faire economy. It also had a very strong appeal to a strong ex-President, and Roosevelt first took his New Nationalism to Osawatomie, Kansas. There, more than half a century before, John Brown had fought his bloody fight against slavery; and there, on August 31, 1910, Roosevelt delivered a thunderous speech endorsing Croly's New Nationalism, which set the needs of the United States before the demands of regional minorities or powerful individuals.

At the Republican Convention in 1912 the incumbent President, William Howard Taft, beloved of business, held onto the nomination. Undaunted, Roosevelt immediately formed the Progressive party, more popularly known as the "Bull Moosers." Their platform promised to make little business big and all business honest, instead of trying to make big business little while allowing it to remain dishonest.

While the Republicans were split between the conservative Taft and the rejuvenated Roosevelt, the Democrats plodded through forty-six convention ballots before nominating a minister's son to whom the trusts seemed downright sinful. Against Roosevelt's New Nationalism, Woodrow Wilson brought a revived call for open competition, which he named the "New Freedom." Taft had nothing new to offer. He could only await defeat with a good grace, and for the first time both leading candidates were reformers. When Wilson proved the winner, Roosevelt Progressives found it easy enough to fall under the sway of Wilson's sermons. The era of reform seemed to have arrived.

Domestic Reform Wilson's ideas were in tune with the times. The spirit of reform had penetrated even to the Supreme Court, with Louis Brandeis's defense of Oregon's ten-hour law. Basically the issue involved the constitutionality of a state limiting the working hours of laundry women to ten hours a day. Joseph Choate had already refused to accept the case, thinking it quite fitting that a hearty washerwoman should contract freely for longer hours if she felt so disposed. Brandeis then took up the case, limiting his discussion of immutable law to a few minutes and concentrating on the purely humane and social issues. This produced a parade of factory inspectors and health experts, whose composite testimony clearly showed that the ten-hour law for women was vital for the protection of their safety and welfare. In a unanimous decision, the Supreme Court held Oregon's law to be constitutional. Not only was this a step toward stronger government control—in that sense more in keeping with Roosevelt than Wilson—it was also a clear victory for reform Darwinism at the highest level.

If this was the prologue, Wilson came on with a vigorous first act. Among his legislative successes were instituting workmen's compensation for federal employees, the Adamson Act decreeing an eight-hour day for interstate railroad workers, the La Follette Act improving the lot of sailors, a federal income tax, and an upswing in workmen's compensation at the state level. As part of the general uplift, women raised their skirts and lobbied clamorously for the right to vote. With state after state granting them suffrage, this was the final victorious assault.

As a direct attack on big business monopolies, Wilson put through the antitrust act that prevented corporations from buying the stock of other companies, thus closing a loophole in the Sherman act. Probably his most lasting contribution in its effect on capitalist economy was his Federal Reserve Act. The great age of the robber barons had known no central bank. It had had its Jay Cookes who went under and its J. P. Morgans who did not, but financially the government had been at the mercy of private money. The idea of the Federal Reserve System came from Germany with Paul M. Warburg, a Hamburg-born banker, and by and large it was a European import. The banking system, in fact, is owned by the members, who are chartered by the federal government, and is supervised by a board of governors who meet in Washington, D.C. State banks may join the system as long as they fulfill certain requirements. The overall effect of this system has been to stabilize finance, to provide against the regional money draft, to minimize fluctuations in the business cycle, and generally to strengthen the government's position, where before it had sat at Morgan's feet.

The road to domestic reform lay open and inviting before Wilson and his disciples and converts. Then Europe went to war, with Germany playing the part of villain, an affront to many progressives, who revered the land where social reform had been born. Roosevelt, who had reveled in San Juan Hill, was already beating a drum and pointing out with dubious logic that to sing "I didn't raise my boy to be a soldier" was the same as singing "I didn't raise my girl to be a mother." Wilson and the other progressives held back, hoping to consolidate and push forward dramatic reform. To prosecute a foreign war, which most reformers saw as nothing but a greedy struggle for wealth and power, would mean catering to big business. Fortunately or unfortunately, Wilson was a missionary and gradually, as the war expanded and Germany's role became more apparent, he began to see the war as one against mankind. Eventually he took the United States into it with the loftiest of motives, to guide a victory that would culminate in world reform and, as he put it, "make the world safe for democracy."

In fact, the war brought on a financial boom. Business was never better, and even American farmers briefly prospered as their farms became the breadbasket of Europe. Wilson's only great defeat was the peace that followed. By then he had concentrated on foreign affairs and domestic reformers had despaired of him. When the Senate barred United States participation in the League of Nations formed at the war's end, Wilson's presidency was destroyed. He lay in the White House, spiritually broken and physically paralyzed, his fondest dream shattered. His successor, Harding, came in on a slogan, "Back to Normalcy," and like so much of Harding, it was a mistake. "Back to normality" was what he'd intended to say, but "Normalcy" turned out to be twice as catchy and a bit more coherent than his advocacy of a stiff protective tariff to help the struggling industries of Europe get back on their feet.

These were the roaring twenties. Woman suffrage had come at last, but it didn't seem, as some had expected, to bring a motherly touch to elections. The direct election of U.S. senators made less difference in a democracy than some had hoped. Except for the farmer who was losing the foreign market, postwar incomes were high and unemployment low. The hero of the decade was Henry Ford, who put the country on wheels. It didn't much matter that he financed an assault on a supposed Jewish conspiracy to rule the world, or that he tried to squirm his way out of a libel suit with an energy born of cowardice. The nation loved him for his Model T, and perhaps with a sort of nostalgia. The old robber barons were gone. A new second-generation corporate capitalism, though bigger than ever, was falling into the hands of managers.

Not only was business booming, however anonymous it was; the federal government was bigger, too, with unrelinquished wartime powers and a new tendency on the part of the public to look to it for leadership. Though the mechanisms had been designed by reformists, they were now in the hands of Harding and his conservatives, who were pleased to find this machinery worked as well against reform as for it. Regulatory commissions were kept and used, such as those established by the Sherman and Clayton antitrust acts. Dollar-a-year business executives who had helped the government during the war in such agencies as the War Industries Board stayed on, shaping a government that favored cooperation between business and government.

Once Harding departed the scene, he was replaced by Coolidge, who advanced this ghost-ridden prosperity by setting up a federal commission over the emerging radio industry, a commission exclusively staffed by corporation men. Secretary of Commerce and later President Herbert Hoover was in complete accord. He was provoked by waste, which he saw in unbridled competition, and wherever possible he encouraged alliances between government, corporations, and the rapidly expanding trade associations.

Meanwhile, the reformers had fled from the Democrats' sinking ship. Though few drowned in the process, they did not find their bedraggled way to shore in the one cohesive body in which they had put to sea. Labor unions, strengthened by the war, centered around the powerful American Federation of Labor. The farmers had more grievances than ever. Negro race-consciousness was on the rise. What reform had lost was unity. At best, the old leaders could hold back the Babbitts and the advance of business, but by and large what remained were special-interest groups, concerned only with their own limited needs. Their separate voices formed no compelling chorus. The Charleston played on a windup phonograph and the chatter of the ticker tape drowned the voices out. Newly sophisticated America, full of Hemingway and bathtub gin, danced and speculated its giddy way up until 1929 and the crash that was heard around the world.

A New Deal
for Reform

The financial crash of October 29, 1929, brought the confusion and panic of an invasion from Mars. As in the gloomy days of 1873, it began with the dumping of millions of shares on the stock exchanges. This time there were no robber barons to stand as beacons in the storm. They, too, were toppling. Few believed it at first, and when the wave of disaster seemingly receded, people began wringing themselves out and speaking of how frightful the depression had been. But this depression was different. It was not like 1907, when J. P. Morgan sat home playing solitaire while Wall Street went mad with fear, then stepped out the next morning to pull everything together. The bankers were as helpless as the industrial corporations.

The Great Depression What caused the Great Depression, which became worldwide? Even today few economists would entirely agree. In part it was a reckoning brought on by World War I that the victors had tried to pay for with reparations rather than reconstruction. In the United States, the stock market crash that began it was augmented by reckless mar-

54

ginal buying. This meant that stock had been purchased with shaky credit rather than with available cash, credit that could not be made good when the chips were down. The very mood of panic, confusion, and fear that set in, if not a triggering force, was certainly a factor in prolonging and deepening the effects. Related causes were the government's failure to control inflation beforehand and its subsequent inability to stimulate the economy in the face of widespread unemployment, business failures, and general despair.

Scapegoats were readily available, but fixing the blame did not bring solutions. After the stock market's total collapse came the breadlines. Three years passed. Fear became hopeless resignation that sank in to the bone. The land of opportunity seemed to be finished. While 13 million unemployed clamored for help, President Hoover waited for the economic balance, so confidently described by the classical economists, to reestablish itself. He was still waiting when the public, grasping at straws, voted him out of office. The most substantial straw involved was Franklin D. Roosevelt.

What Roosevelt had in abundance was exuberant confidence. He had no patience with intellectuals or theorists. Trial and error was his approach, and if it failed, he was ready to try again. He had great admiration for his cousin, Teddy, who had endorsed a new nationalism without ever giving it a try, and this in the beginning was the skeleton upon which his pragmatic New Deal was fleshed out.

Inauguration Day in 1933 was cold and gray. The banks were about to close for a so-called four-day holiday, and a tattered Wall Street was silent. The economic heart of the country scarcely beat as Roosevelt, the crippled President of a crippled land, jutted out his jaw and announced that the only fear to be overcome was fear itself.

The New Deal   Thus began the most frantic one hundred days that peacetime Washington has ever known. Before the bank holiday was over, emergency banking legislation had been prepared and had passed both houses of Congress. Hoover had feared that the use of federal funds for unemployment relief would ruin the character of recipients. At the same time, he thought it would violate the immutable economic law that the national debt cannot go beyond a certain point without bankrupting the government. In the long run, he may have been right, but at the same time such a philosophy seemed a course without end. Unemployment had become a problem too immense for the states and the cities to cope with. The burden of debt on farmers and householders was promptly eased with federal credit.

Roosevelt's chief aid and dispenser of largesse at the time was Harry Hopkins, of whom it was said that he sat down at his desk in the hall while waiting for the paint to dry in his office and in less than two hours had spent $5 million. The economic merit of Roosevelt's schemes are still being debated. What he undeniably brought to a disillusioned nation was confidence and hope, and by the end of those one hundred days these qualities had been transmitted to both farm and factory. In the congressional elections of 1934, the Democratic party increased its majority, which amounted to an almost-unheard-of vote of confidence in an off-year election.

Even big business was anxious for a helping hand, and Franklin Roosevelt had something in mind that initially was very like his cousin's New Nationalism. It was based on his notion that businessmen had a social responsibility beyond mere profit-making, and so the National Recovery Administration (NRA) was born. Ideally, the NRA was designed to prime the economic and industrial pump. In addition to extensive federal public-works programs, industry was allowed to draw up new cooperative plans through trade associations. Antitrust legislation was suspended. Prices could be fixed by industry. Only over the codes relating to hours, wages, and conditions of competition was there direct federal supervision. Envisioned was a partnership of government, industry, and labor working together to increase employment, stabilize wages, and boost output.

On its surface, the NRA smacked of socialism. In actual practice, it moved toward Mussolini's idea of the fascist corporate state, which will be examined presently. Early dissenters began to say the initials stood for National Run Around. Small businesses were being destroyed. Finally, in May of 1935, when a poultry concern wanted to know whether it was proper for a federal code to tell it which chickens could be killed and how much they had to pay their chicken-killers, the Supreme Court declared the NRA unconstitutional. Of Roosevelt's experiments, none ended up with a worse name than the NRA, which raised prices faster than wages and led the President to the disgruntled conclusion that Wilson had sized businessmen up more accurately than had his cousin Teddy.

The United States had begun as a nation of small farmers, a condition that Jefferson had appreciated and encouraged. But those good old days were long gone. Even as late as 1850, two-thirds of the work force had been employed in agriculture, but the Civil War brought the industrial age. Despite the opening of the West, there came a growing urban drift and a slow decline in the farming population, which has today shrunk to little more than 5 percent of the total population, and that group has completely changed its character. The small farmer, associated with an air of peace and plenty, with enough for himself and some left over, has given way to extremes: the bare subsistence farming typified by Appalachia, and the vast commercial farm worked by hired hands.

The depression hurt farmers rich and poor, and the Agricultural Adjustment Act (AAA) was designed to raise food prices by reducing farm surplus. Farmers were induced to take land out of production, burn crops, and slaughter stock. On the face of it, this was a shocking procedure while much of the world was literally starving to death. Within a few months of the NRA decision the experiment ended with a Supreme Court decree invalidating the act. A soil-bank program encouraged farmers with subsidies to turn crop-producing land into pasture: another failure. The problem here was that only the big farmer who could afford to take his worst land out of production was helped. While collecting subsidies on this fallow land, he would meanwhile build up production on his remaining acreage with improved seed and fertilizer. Meanwhile, the small farmer, who could barely make ends meet by using every inch of available land, collected nothing at all. Things went so far that a country club felt free to apply for soil-bank money for not planting cotton on its golf course.

The Tennessee Valley Authority The most successful and lasting of the early New Deal programs was the Tennessee Valley Authority. The Tennessee River, fifth largest in the country, had always been hampered as a navigable waterway by its rapid and rough drop at Muscle Shoals, Alabama. During World War I, the government had planned to build nitrate factories at this point, as well as a dam to supply hydroelectric power to run the factories. The war's end diminished the need for nitrate and the factories were left unfinished, though the Wilson dam was subsequently completed there, leaving the government with a not very practical $100 million investment, a veritable white elephant.

Then came Roosevelt with his desire to put idle hands to work in the hope that the regional economy would be stimulated. In the spring of 1933, the Tennessee Valley Authority was created as a regional agency of the federal government. Technically it was a public corporation but with many private aspects, empowered to control floods, make the river navigable, and produce and market electric power. Along with the NRA and the AAA, its constitutionality was questioned before the Supreme Court in the case of *Ashwander* v. *TVA*. In 1936, its constitutionality was upheld.

CAPITALISM

Eventually the TVA would operate over thirty major dams, build navigation locks into its principal dams, and encourage local government and private business to develop port facilities. The result was that river commerce increased a hundredfold. The authority's most controversial undertaking, the marketing of electric power, was bitterly resisted by privately owned power companies. At first, the authority limited output to turbines installed in the big dams and joined with local units to supply wholesale power for distribution. Then private companies were slowly bought up until TVA became in fact a regional monopoly. Critics alleged that the TVA could sell power more cheaply because it was not subject to taxation, and in this economic advantage there is a parallel to be seen with Rockefeller's railroad rebates. Other functions of the TVA included the operation of the nitrate plants at Muscle Shoals and the development of recreation areas and reclamation of the area's forests.

The TVA is undeniably socialism, but socialism at its functional best. Some critics saw it as an opening wedge. Actually, it has proved more of a yardstick for forcing private utility companies to improve service and lower prices through its competition, a process that showed that profits could thus be increased since enlarged use more than compensated for lower rates. Here, indeed, the New Nationalism was a success. It showed how, under ideal conditions, the federal government could work in consort with local units, both public and private, while developing the multiple possibilities of an area as a harmonious whole. India's Damodar Valley development program and Colombia's Cauca River project have both been undertaken on the TVA model, not to mention other river-basin programs in the United States.

Basically the TVA survived not because it was constitutional, but because it worked. The AAA and the NRA went under because they didn't bring about sufficient results. The net outcome of these three programs, along with Roosevelt's other experiments, though raising some hopes, did not pull the nation out of a worldwide depression of a magnitude unknown since Europe had paid the price for the Napoleonic wars. With the NRA and the AAA gone, Roosevelt was unabashedly ready to try something else. The NRA experience had convinced him that big business lacked public spirit and made an uncooperative partner in working for recovery. This conviction and the fact that Senator Huey Long, the demagogical ex-governor of Louisiana, was threatening to run for President and give the money moguls a good thrashing in the process combined to push Roosevelt farther left of center. From the New Nationalism, which didn't seem to work except on the Tennessee River, he leaned toward Wilson's New Freedom. This change in policy was made very clear by the National Labor Relations Act (the Wagner Act) and the Fair Labor Standards Act, which fixed maximum hours and minimum wages when business failed to do so voluntarily.

Since the Revolution, the two events that most disturbed and altered American society as a whole have been the Civil War and the depression of the 1930s. While the Civil War boosted capitalism toward new heights, the depression nearly finished it off. In Europe, many capitalist countries began to turn wholly or in part to a socialistic solution. In the United States, individual desperation was such that government involvement was welcomed, and this enlarged government activity has never been relinquished. The change has had its gloomy critics and its enthusiastic spokesmen, and it has brought about the most dramatic innovations in economic theory since Adam Smith set down what for so long seemed the immutable laws of capitalist economy.

The thinking behind the new economics really began around the turn of the century in Sweden with the writings of John Gustav Knut Wicksell. He contradicted Say's Law of Markets, which, as has already been seen, alleged there could be no such thing as general overproduction because an equilibrium will always occur in the long run between supply and demand. In Wicksell's view, supply and demand did not need to be automatically self-balancing. This concept, if correct, cut the foundations from under classical theory, which had been developed in a much older and less complex world.

John Maynard Keynes   Wicksell's writings received scant attention, but not so those of John Maynard Keynes. Born in England in 1883, Keynes seemed predestined to be an economist. His father was one of the classical school, and his mother, a graduate of Cambridge, became the lord mayor of that town. As a member of the British treasury department during the First World War, Keynes attended the peace conference after the war and joined the losing minority in an appeal against the reparations heaped on Germany. His frustration at the final terms resulted in his book *The Economic Consequences of the Peace,* which predicted economic disaster for Europe. A shift in British policy back onto the gold standard in 1925 sharpened his expectation of the serious depression that took four more years to develop.

With conditions moving from bad to worse in 1929, Keynes formulated his major thesis presented in *The General Theory of Employment, Interest and Money.* It was not published, however, until 1936, when the New Deal was already well along. Then attention was immediate, for it was the first coherent economic study to fit the times, just as Smith's *Wealth of Nations* had done in its own day.

Keynesian Economics   Keynes' theory was not a refutation of classical economics, particularly as their laws functioned during good times, but it did deny certain hitherto sacrosanct principles and offer means to deal with depression beyond simple faith and patience. His primary quarrel, following Wicksell's lead, was with Say's law. Depressions, according to Say's thinking, were nothing but the self-correcting motion of the economic seesaw in both the goods and labor market. Like sellers who could not market their products, laborers simply had to reduce their salary demands for a customer, in this case an employer, to show up.

Already World War I had brought into question the validity of a complete laissez-faire system. The war had been too big for government not to get involved in production. The Soviet Union, an extreme case, in taking over from Czarist Russia offered a complete reversal of classical economics of a conservative persuasion.

Keynes preferred an updated capitalism to communism. He called attention to the flaw in Say's principle by stating that demand may, in fact, fall short of supply at a level of production and income that corresponds to full employment. At least, in the short run of history this could be the case, and to place confidence in the long run of Say's reasoning seemed to Keynes to be saying, "In the long run we all are dead."

Then, too, he did not subscribe to the idea that a laborer, simply by reducing his wage demand, would eventually find work. Unemployment was rather a result in the falling off of consumer demand. Keynes saw income flowing in a rough circle; the manufacturing of a product, its selling, and the buying of it. A fall in demand and hence unemployment were a result of the drying up of this circulatory system, which meant that somewhere along the line money was being withheld. This money was being saved. The classicists had assumed that all savings were spent by those investing in business, but Keynes believed that very often people will hoard their money rather than invest it. Such hoarding has the self-perpetuating effect of causing the entire economic structure to stagnate. Depression will result, and Keynes' answer to the problem was to get hoarded money back into the economic flow by encouraging spending and investment. This action can be helped by lowering interest rates to make saving less profitable which in turn makes investment in new business more attractive.

When a capitalist economy is in balance and business is good, there is very little need for Keynes or for government activity, but during extremes, particularly during depressions, most economists and politicians agree there is need for both. Government, as Keynes saw it, could leave the economy free to respond to the decisions of individual consumers and producers, involving itself only to help maintain competition and support a healthy level of investment and employment. Should income and employment begin to fall, the central bank could manipulate the supply of money by reducing interest rates. A more drastic step, already initiated pragmatically by Roosevelt, was for the government to spend vast sums on public works, thereby putting money into circulation.

An increase in the money supply, brought about by lowered interest rates, would encourage consumers to shop, industry to invest, and so on. Conversely, in times of inflation, the government should try to counteract rising prices by influencing people to save money, thereby creating a surplus for use during a deflationary trend. Each dollar spent or withheld in this way represents more than its face value in terms of national income, for one dollar of relief, as an example, might proceed from the welfare recipient as a dollar to the retail food store, then to the wholesaler, next to the farmer, and so on around the economic circle. Public works in this way could become the equivalent of war as a stimulant to the economy.

As a parallel device, Keynes favored stiff progressive taxation for the economy as a whole, combined with social insurance and public services in order to redistribute the income. He had more in mind than playing Robin Hood, for he felt that investment was not encouraged by a large number of poorly paid people at one end of the scale and a small group of very rich at the other. This situation approximated in theory the condition of many underdeveloped countries, with the poor existing near subsistence level unable to provide enough demand to attract investment, while the wealthy could afford too great savings. In this he agreed with Marx, whose theory was less clearly articulated. To be healthy, then, a nation requires, according to Keynes, a more nearly equal distribution of wealth, and such has been the tendency in capitalistic countries throughout the modern world.

Keynes has been accused by his enemies of being a totalitarian planner, from fascist to socialist. Yet, basically, his contribution has been enlightened capitalism. He has been blamed for putting the world back on a mercantile course by encouraging trade barriers between countries. But he has accepted responsibility for this hindrance to international laissez-faire as the only way to get at the more basic problems of unemployment and depression within the great nations upon whom the others depend for both foreign markets and capital. However much he has been criticized and however much the good old days are lamented, Keynesian theory was seized upon by the young generation of New Deal American economists to justify the already existing policies of public works and deficit spending. With subsequent prosperity, he has not been abandoned and may be held, whether for good or bad, almost solely responsible for the basic economic policies of the last thirty years.

Of course, as far as the New Deal itself was concerned, Keynesian theory came only as a vindicating afterthought. There are those who would quarrel even with this, saying that by and large the New Deal measures retarded the economy, that business, indeed, would have made its own recovery, perhaps faster. The upswing seemed to be under way in 1936, with some giving credit to NRA and as many others attributing the improvement to NRA's death. By mid-1937, the optimistic glow had faded. Production began to slide, and about all that the New Deal had left to show on the credit side was Roosevelt's undaunted confidence. There was a renewal of deficit government spending in the second half of 1937 and in 1938.

Throughout this period, despite the Communist dogma to

the effect that capitalist prosperity requires a wartime economy, there had been no resort to the building of an armament industry. Other depressed countries, not so much for the economy's sake as because they wanted war, were investing heavily in arms. This was particularly true of Germany, Italy, and Japan. The coming of war, of course, was a kill-or-cure measure, and most national economies thrived unless they were bombed to bits. The United States, as in the past, had no such bad luck. Business picked up during World War II, leaving the final record of the New Deal a murky one. Would prosperity have returned anyway? Had the New Deal experiments helped? Was recovery all thanks to the war? This is a debate that has never been resolved and probably never will be, but, nevertheless, the spirit of government had changed drastically, a change that the war would accentuate.

World War II Roosevelt had none of Wilson's doubts about involvement in a European war, nor did most of the liberals of the day. There was little of the old-time hysteria. Very few bands marched to send the boys off, and no one suggested changing the name of sauerkraut to "liberty cabbage." Although the fighting went on in Europe for over two years before the United States officially declared war in December, 1941, Roosevelt had been backing Britain since March of that year with lend-lease. Once Pearl Harbor had resolved the last strong opposition to war, Roosevelt could speak of replacing Old Doctor New Deal with Young Doctor Win-the-War. Young Doctor Win-the-War was dressed like a conservative businessman. In the election of 1942, many New Dealers lost out in Congress, and the economy was booming. The sheer momentum of American arms production doomed the Axis from the start. It was only a matter of time.

While Roosevelt would make his mistakes internationally, as Wilson had done, he was aware of the disruption that wartime inflation had caused in the First World War, and of its consequences after the armistice. This time inflation was limited by rationing and price controls. Savings built up. The tax structure followed a Keynesian blueprint, paying for the emergency system as debts arose. With the war's end, people had money, and the slump in munitions spending was balanced by a catch-up boom in desired consumer goods. The smooth transition was also helped by the sad fact of the Cold War, which allowed no complete return to a peacetime economy.

The country was healthy. It had survived the greatest depression that the world had ever known and it had thrived on the greatest war. It had lived with, and learned to love or hate, the most inventive President the people had ever elected. Now Roosevelt was dead, but the United States was set on a new course. Classical, self-regulating laissez-faire capitalism was gone. The depression had hit the American public over the head. The blow had not been quite fatal, but it had changed the national mentality. More than a government that would free every man's opportunity, the majority of the public wanted a government that would guarantee every man's security. From faith in self-adjusting markets and the business community, they had turned to wanting protection from the disruptive forces inherent in industry and an entirely market-oriented economy. This meant heavy taxes, unemployment insurance, social security, workmen's compensation, and federal grants in aid of education. Whether this welfarism and economic security will release great individual energies that will more than compensate for the financial, social, and psychological costs involved, or whether it leads to mediocrity and the stultifying of initiative, or whether, in fact, it follows some less certain middle course, remains to be seen.

Another Road:
Totalitarian Capitalism

The Second World War not only altered democratic capitalism, it nipped in the bud a vicious aberration of it. In the 1930s and '40s fascism, or what can be called totalitarian capitalism, posed to democratic capitalism the same sort of threat that communism poses to democratic socialism today. Though full-fledged fascism died in the war, it is still a theoretical alternative to democratic capitalism. Particularly, it is a polarizing response to communism or, more especially, socialism, which has made more actual gains even in the United States than most conservative capitalists care to admit.

Italian Fascism   Because vestiges of the fascist system are still found in the world today and because "fascist" is a popular and foggy epithet to hurl at politicians, policemen, or almost any political opponent, its history will be briefly reviewed here. Fascism was born in a politically tumultuous Italy following World War I. The name was derived from the Latin word *fasces,* literally "bundles," which referred to the framework of rods surrounding an ax that was carried before Ancient Roman magistrates as a symbol of authority. The *fasces* represented strength through unity.

Fascism was founded by Benito Mussolini, whose first name was given him in honor of Benito Juarez, the Mexican revolutionary. In due time, Mussolini would respond more readily to "il Duce," "the Leader," but his road to fascism was a tortuous one. In World War I he moved from antiwar socialism to a militant position that led him into a duel with a former pacifist Socialist friend. Mussolini lost the duel, but not his life. Recovered from his wound, he had no better success as a soldier, for a training grenade put him out of action before he ever saw the enemy. Now that neither the Socialists nor the army wanted him, he had to dream up something of his own, and that creation turned out to be fascism.

Fascism was founded in Milan in 1919, seemingly with few prospects and fewer votes in the elections. However, among Italian industrialists an unreal fear existed then that Socialists might try to seize power as the Communists had done in Russia. Mussolini encouraged that fear while building up youth squads, his blackshirt army. By 1921 the young movement was off to a head-knocking start in Italy, having within the first six months of that year destroyed fifty-nine chambers of labor (union halls), twenty-five people's centers, eighty-five agrarian cooperatives, and forty-three unions of agricultural workers, not to mention scores of leftist presses and newspapers.

Another year, and Mussolini was moving his improvised army from Naples to Milan, then finally, without any real opposition, to Rome, where the cabinet had resigned in alarm. The king felt obliged to call upon Mussolini to form a new one. Within four years, all rival parties had vanished from the scene and Mussolini was il Duce over all of Italy. The trains ran on time and there were those who loved Mussolini for the order he brought to the country, but the businessmen who had given him initial support found themselves being hemmed into a corporate state in which the Fascists directed everything as in a strictly run trade union. Initially, Mussolini had tried to enlist the favor of his capitalists. Not until the depression did he fully develop the corporate state idea, which drew on the old merchant guild experience of Genoa and Venice. Related occupations were pulled into syndicates that were centralized into provincial unions and finally into a federal group. Employers and employees became organized into a strict military-type hierarchy under a ministry of corporations.

Apart from the fact that the worker was kept strictly in his place while the capitalist remained at the top, the setup of fascism was curiously suggestive of communism. No longer was the economy subject to the automatic regulations of supply and demand. Prices were fixed by the government and quotas set, but even these strict controls, coupled with incessant harangues about the glorious legions of ancient Rome, failed to generate a spirited mechanized army. Mussolini's conquests were economic disasters, and in 1936 he made his final mistake. He threw in Italy's lot with Nazi Germany. From that point, the path led always down: military defeat, rejection by his people, then resuscitation for a time as a deflated Nazi puppet. Finally the end came where it had all begun. In Milan he was hung upside down in Piazza Loreto, the virile profile that had so often honored photographers beaten beyond recognition.

The Nature of Fascism So much for Italian fascism. It had endured for a decade before another form of fascism took hold in Germany, the rise of which was so meteoric that Mussolini became little more than a ludicrous, tag-along clown. Although its name is Italian, history will always first associate fascism with Nazi Germany and its leader, Adolf Hitler. Before moving to the German experience, a few common elements must be indicated in order to distinguish modern fascism from other less lethal forms of tyranny, for fascism is in fact more than simple dictatorship or totalitarian capitalism.

In the first place, it is a popular movement with massive national support. That support is directed toward one charismatic leader who represents a particular nation. The nation is all-important. It has a life of its own that transcends that of the individual. Various devices were employed by both Mussolini and Hitler to foster individual submersion in this sense of nationhood. Old glories and old gods were revived; in the case of Germany, the Nordic gods and the warriors who worshiped them, all for the greater glory of the Fatherland. Even the leaders were depersonalized: il Duce, der Führer, and so forth. Not only has such a nation a past, but a purpose, a destiny that inevitably, within the fascist context, means expansion into empire. Designated enemies both within the nation and without served a vital purpose. An atmosphere of "struggle" is encouraged, a word beloved by Fascists and Communists alike. The struggle dependably begins against the negative elements within the state itself. In Italy these were the Socialists and Communists and, in the end, anyone who resisted the single-minded progress of the party. With internal resistance crushed, the Fascist state would inevitably move on to enemies without.

Fascism regarded communism, with its messianic vigor, as its chief foe from the start. Communism would in due course accept the challenge. It had no choice in fact or in theory, for it pictured fascism as capitalism's last stand against the Communist tide. Rather than a last stand, Mussolini preferred to think of fascism as a religious crusade, though he acknowledged no god above the state.

For its fruition, fascism may have needed the twentieth century, with its radios and its loudspeakers, and above all its widespread economic disaster. By 1932 the Great Depression had reached a culmination, and there was vast, worldwide unemployment. Throughout Germany, wages were cut in half without tax reduction. From top to bottom, German society was stricken. The landed aristocracy, known as the Junkers, had been used to running the state. They had never favored a democratic government, which would fail to recognize their inherent superiority. Then, too, they feared the power of the growing industrialists. The industrialists, in turn, opposed the trade unions, which, with reason, they regarded as communistic and therefore anxious to redistribute whatever wealth remained. The German middle class also had its fears, particularly the prospect of being overtaken by the mass of workers as they watched prices skyrocket above salaries and saw hard-earned investment security become worthless paper.

Nazism Any nation will seek out a strong leader in troubled times, particularly a nation that has relied on authoritarian leadership in the past. Taking some tips from the already well-established Mussolini, Hitler characterized himself simply as the "Führer," the leader first of the Nazis (a name contracted from the German word for National Socialists), and then as the personification of the German nation. "You are mine, and I am yours," became a popularized slogan. Hitler had appeals for all and he offered visions of a new social order, different and often contradictory visions to suit different tastes.

For the soldier, there was the honest purpose of making Germany strong; the "mighty-sword" vision. For the Junkers and the industrialists, there was Hitler's pledge that "Down with Capitalism" chants were only meant to get workmen on the job, and there was the promise of massive military contracts. The middle class was told that Jewish "stock-exchange bandits" would be gotten rid of and international capitalism would be prevented from further milking Germany. To the worker, he offered free education and a society, as exemplified by the Nazi party, that would tend toward classlessness. In general, these pledges to the working class were not believed. Communist workers remained true to their faith until the Nazi stick replaced words, to bring them into line.

The German peasants, however, were flattered by the notion that they were the backbone of the state. They were promised that foreign competition would end. Further, they were led to hope that the great estates would be confiscated and that they would replace the Junkers as landowners. Frustrated youth was given its cause at last. They were called the hope of the future, the architects of the one-thousand-year reich (or empire) to come. Even women were appealed to as a group with the tenuous logic that once the Nazis had stabilized the economy and provided general security, men would be more inclined to marry.

As a persuader, Hitler has never had an equal. To gain support, he relied on symbols, slogans, and pure emotion, rather than logic or sound reasoning. With a basic contempt for the average German, he believed that the lazy mind could best be aroused by oratory. He had less confidence in the written word, which upon cool examination could prove the illogic of many of his favorite themes. He preferred vast mass meetings to give a feeling of belonging—of great importance to a people whose traditions lay in ruins.

The swastika party flag was everywhere; white and black for the imperial colors, red for the Socialists and for blood— blood for Germany, blood that the party had spilt in the revolution that failed. The key to it all was blood: "Blood and Iron" etched on the blades of the Hitler Youth, pure Aryan blood to encourage thinking with the blood and never with the brain. It was, in fact, Hitler's goal to turn his people into a flock of "bloodthirsty sheep," and he succeeded to the point of gaining 37 percent of the popular vote in the summer elections of 1932.

The Nazis never did better in a popular election. They didn't need to, for their political opponents were divided among themselves. Besides, the old president, General von Hindenburg, was dying. What could not be accomplished by persuasion could now be achieved by terror. Destroying domestic communism was of first importance. Communists were imprisoned. The unions, largely Communist in spirit, were forbidden to strike, while an alliance between the party and the big capitalists moved toward the sort of corporate state already established in Italy.

Herein, however, lay considerable difference, for Italy lacked the raw materials and industrial development vital to big business. In Germany, however, this was not the case, and industry was larger and much more powerful. It was also in league with the military in a secret arms program long before Hitler came to power. These two groups, industry and the military, were vital to Hitler's plans and strong enough not to be bullied at first. His overtures were greeted with a certain contempt. After all, he was an Austrian of dubious birth, low military rank, and had no formal education beyond secondary school; but by 1932 he was addressing the industry club and receiving campaign contributions. An early capitalist disciple was Fritz Thyssen, the German coal baron, who remained a solid supporter of Hitler's until the cynical Nazi pact with Russia. At that point, Thyssen denounced his protégé, lost his industrial empire, and ended up in an Italian detention camp with nothing left except a conscience somewhat less tarnished than those of his associates.

As the German economy began to move, primarily owing to arms production, Hitler initiated his takeover. He started at the bottom with labor, breaking up the unions and supervising all of life's activities via the so-called Strength Through Joy movement, which even planned the workers' infrequent vacations. After labor came the small businesses. By 1937, all minor corporations had to dissolve. Stockholder power was gradually reduced by building up nazified boards of directors. Only the giant capitalists were to profit, those who cooperated with Hitler. The program was achieved by strict control of the workers, an official lowering of the wage rate, higher tariffs, and the award of profitable contracts for expanded public-works projects. As World War II developed, the minimal cost of labor decreased, for workers joined the armies and prisoners took their places. Germany became a monstrous robber-baron heaven, except for the allied bombers and the possibility of going to Dachau if one forgot to say "Heil Hitler."

The Krupps   A synonym for German capitalism through the ages has been Krupp, and the Krupp role did not change with Hitler or his war. The powerful Krupp family had begun making arms and armor soon after Arndt Krupp had joined the merchants guild in Essen in 1587. At the time of World War I, the family and the business were headed by Gustav Krupp von Bohlen und Halbach who had married the Krupp heiress, Bertha, for whom the Paris gun, "Big Bertha," was named. For them, the war did not end in 1918. It smoldered on, fanned by the sight of British soldiers supervising the destruction of the great armament factories in 1920, and the killing of several workers three years later, after they had turned steam jets on a French patrol.

Gustav was a remarkable man. Dapper, even dainty, he was conspicuously shorter than his wife. His family called him Taffy, but his business rivals feared him. To be always on the alert, he kept his offices at a temperature of fifty-five degrees and spent his leisure moments checking railroad timetables for mistakes. Fortunately for Hitler, Krupp was fiercely patriotic, with a ready loyalty for any national German leader. As his sons and relations were killed off during the Second World War, he had the evident solace of knowing they had died for the Führer.

Gustav Krupp's plans for Germany had predated Hitler's prominence. In the early twenties, he was already working out details with the army for the ostensible production of agricultural equipment: light, medium, and heavy tractors, the latter curiously equipped to carry 7.5 cm cannon. Production was further disguised by opening plants in other European countries. The greatest irony of all was the fact that one big gun factory was situated in Holland at The Hague, virtually within sight of the International Court of Justice in the Peace Palace, a contribution of another less bellicose capitalist, Andrew Carnegie. Only slightly less ironic was the testing of the new weapons, carried out near Moscow with the Soviet blessing.

Krupp was not an early convert to Hitler. He would have preferred to have the kaiser back, and his wife in no uncertain terms regarded Hitler as an "ill-bred guttersnipe." Krupp was less blunt, referring to the Nazi leader as "that certain gentleman." If he were only Adolf von Hitler, with a bit of Prussian nobility in his closet! By 1930, however, Hitler was becoming a force, and he courted Krupp with the thought of putting down the Communists and suppressing independent labor unions at the same time. The militant Left was a genuine if minor threat, and Krupp finally, in 1932, went over to Hitler, maintaining his sense of dignity by saying he'd "hired" the Nazi leader. The following year Krupp was giving gigantic campaign pledges to finance the terror election, in which Hitler seized complete power.

With the developing Fascist corporate-state idea, Krupp became the official director of business, thus linking big business with the Nazi party. This action was responsive to the "leadership principle," which also justified sending labor leaders to concentration camps. Thus absolute leadership was restored to the employer, giving him the power that had been held by nineteenth-century capitalists, but with one great difference. Though the employer led, and the biggest employer led other employers, Krupp still found himself under Hitler's thumb, a position he did not seem to mind. He had become a servant without knowing it, and, despite his wife's disgust, he regarded Hitler as infallible. But Gustav Krupp von Bohlen und Halbach was growing old, and senile too. Before the war was over, he would lie deranged and helpless in a vast hunting lodge set in the Austrian Alps (where Barbarossa is also said to sleep).

With Gustav's withdrawal from the scene, the firm's actual head throughout the war years was Alfried Felix Alwyn Krupp von Bohlen und Halbach: "Krupp" for short. He would, at the war's end, spend five years in prison, but during the war itself he would have a robber-baron's field day sufficient to make even Jay Gould blush. By 1935 Hitler had already renounced the restrictions of the Versailles Treaty regarding armament limitation. Foreign operations were closed down, but the smokestacks of the factories in Essen, fed from the black, coal-laden bowels of the earth below them, were darkening the skies of western Germany. Never before had such deadly tools been produced at such a rate. As soon as these weapons were successfully used in Poland, France, and the Balkans, Alfried Krupp, in cooperation with the army, was encouraged to expand his steel empire. Conquests were such that Alfried toured Europe in a private fighter plane, taking over likely factories. Occasionally minor compensation was offered to the former owner, who took it and smiled, or got nothing. In any case, Alfried got the factory. At first there was some effort to hide this piracy behind a veil of buying or leasing the properties, but as the war worsened, open seizure was the rule.

Krupp was the biggest capitalist the world had ever known, with an empire spreading through twelve countries, with mines in Russia, Greece, Norway, Yugoslavia, and France, and with shipyards in the Netherlands. Before the end of the war, there was a formal decree making Alfried Krupp owner of all. That was as of December 15, 1943. By then, Jewish and Russian prisoners were manning the factories, on no pay, poor food, and only barbed wire between them and the allied bombers. A few dug themselves ditches as bomb shelters, but the Jews were not even permitted that much protection. At best, they could burrow into slag heaps with their bare hands.

Fascism Today   This was Fascist capitalism gone mad, part of a bad dream from which the world has awakened, hopefully with enough remembrance to avoid future recurrence. There are many who predict a Fascist future for the United States. They point to the clenched fist so often raised by the Black Panthers and frequently painted on walls. There, at least, is a symbol, but of course the Panthers are an infinitesimal group. Also, they are turned, as are most other young militants, toward the Left and away from the establishment, the group that ordinarily would gain from fascism. What about a Fascist backlash, then? The provocation from students and blacks seems hardly to demand such a strong reaction. United States police forces, no matter how maligned, are no blackshirt army, and yet they keep order. Then there is the long democratic tradition, as well established in the United States as the authoritarian mold was in Germany. The very nature of the two-party political system inhibits a leader's drifting toward extremes.

Some other countries are perhaps more vulnerable. Since the late 1930s, Spain has existed under a government professing fascism. It has the dictator and the strict economic controls, particularly regarding labor, requisite to a Fascist system; but it lacks the national fervor and the warlike sense of mission that distinguish true fascism from other totalitarian regimes. More recently, South Africa has been described as fascistic, and again some of the elements are present: suppression of part of its population, in this case the black majority; control of the courts; strict censorship; hostility toward the world in general; symptoms that when added up amount more to a cornered white imperialism, than to expansive fascism.

Peace and the Welfare State

In the United States, World War II was over and the great experimenter was dead. Prices were going up. The Congress was fighting over price controls and many of the aging New Dealers were in rout. The Eightieth Congress killed most rent control and drastically trimmed allocations for crop storage and soil conservation. Over all now hung the specter of atomic war. As many democratic liberals went over to Henry Wallace, because he reminded them of Roosevelt and reform, the party that had had its own way so long grimly anticipated Thomas Dewey and the end of welfarism.

The Postwar Economy The victory of Truman and the Democratic party in 1948 wasn't the country's only surprise. Many experts had expected an economic setback after the war. The first reaction, however, was an outpouring of liquid funds. Cash, bank savings, government bonds were all spent for those luxuries of living, such as new cars, that had been unobtainable in wartime. Prices climbed. Theoretically it couldn't last, and yet the boom went on well into the 1950s as the urban population spread into the suburbs. Even the great tax burden of the defense establishment couldn't stop the country's economic growth.

The phenomenon extended to ravaged Europe. Remembering the lesson of World War I and fearing a Communist takeover, the United States at first underwrote the vanquished countries. Thanks to the importation of American money, methods, and mass production they revived. According to time-honored theories, Germany was economically doomed. In communist dogma, capitalism needed a big armaments industry and the lifeblood of colonies abroad to nourish chronic economic anemia in the mother country. Germany no longer had either and, disproving communist doctrine, it was largely for these reasons that she recovered so rapidly. Similarly, before the war Japan had become bogged down in a colonial empire that had proved a parasitic growth on her own economy and had diverted her from the rich European and North American markets. Defeat buried her dreams of world empire, but it freed her great industrial potential from burdensome armaments.

Conversely, the winners did not progress so rapidly. Britain retained a vast world empire and military obligations abroad. In part because of her close ties with the internationally minded United States, she was reluctant to surrender these obligations. She has been accused of not realizing that Queen Victoria was long since dead, but most Britons were aware that the old days were gone forever. Only with the casting aside of these dubious international "fruits of victory" has Britain's economy experienced an upswing.

France, half winner, half loser, appropriately followed a middle path. After World War I, she had sat on her moldering Maginot Line, hoping that reparations from Germany would fill the holes in her war-damaged economy. In fact, the reparation system kept the German economy so unhealthy that the effect was contagious throughout Europe. Even France suffered. There was no Maginot Line after World War II and virtually no reparations, but France found herself held back by two colonial wars, one in Algeria and another in Indochina. The latter she gave up only after a defeat. De Gaulle, in his wisdom, let Algeria go, too, although only after considerable bloodshed, along with other French interests in Africa. With the sword broken, France, too, saw economic health return.

While Europe seems for the time being to have learned that modern war can profit no one and has taken the path of prosperity and peace, there remain doubts about the United States. Hopefully, she has been instructed by the tragedy of foreign wars, and, short of war itself, by the economically wasting attempt to police the entire world.

The first post–World War II policeman–President was Harry Truman. Domestically he spoke like a militant reformer: higher minimum wage, wider social security, tougher antitrust action. With his election to his own term in 1948, achieved by his own efforts, rather than succeeding to the departed Roosevelt's uncompleted term, it seemed that his "Fair Deal" program would have smooth sailing, for most Americans had come to accept massive government involvement in the economy. Construction and the baby boom in these years made for fair economic weather. The Korean War, when it came, gave an apparent lift, though the war was small enough not to focus the entire economy upon winning it. With taxation as the only control, the result was a rapid World War I-type inflation. As the fighting dragged on indecisively, Western Europe won the real victories by closing the dollar gap and the trade deficit with huge exports. Through peace and prosperity, economic stability has moved Western Europe into the position of being a world power center equal in stature to the United States and the Soviet Union.

Truman dared not escalate and could not seem to end the Korean War. It was time for a change, and the first Republican

President in twenty years, Dwight D. Eisenhower. In the twentieth century, economic reform and the conducting of wars had been entirely in Democratic hands. The Republicans had come to be termed "do-nothings," but Eisenhower began well enough. He ended the Korean War, went on to mitigate the war in Egypt, and to avoid involvement in Hungary. Domestically, however, he was more of a do-nothing than even the Democrats might have expected.

Throughout his administration, Eisenhower retained close ties with the opposition party and infuriated his own more conservative colleagues by not moving to repeal economic programs of past Democratic administrations. Eisenhower's main concern was the country's economy, the limitation of inflation, and the waste inherent in the huge military budget. His approach to military spending was to cut off cash disbursements by the armed services against current and future obligations. Twenty-five private contractors were informed by the Defense Department in 1957 that it had simply run out of funds. At the same time, having accepted Keynesian methods of manipulating the economy, the Federal Reserve held back funds from banks from whom loans otherwise could have been obtained. The Korean War had strained the national economy. Now Eisenhower's well-intended efforts were frightening it. Then along came the first Russian sputnik, and, as a matter of pride, the government was off once again on a spending spree.

The nation as a whole had not been displeased with these Republican years. They had given the country a rest. The narrow victory in 1960 of a Democratic administration seems to have been due to the personal appeal of one candidate over the other. But John Kennedy came with great promise, high hopes, and, in keeping with Democratic tradition, a slogan: "the New Frontier." As far as the economic disposition of his short-lived New Frontier was concerned, it adhered closely to the Keynesian formula. Basic to the democratic way of life was the freedom of the community to express its preference through an unrestricted marketplace, and the state's function was not to dominate but only to operate a mechanism of checks and balances to ensure the general welfare. The methods employed would be manipulation of the interest rate, with the government spending or not spending as the times seem to demand, and adjustment of taxation.

Although this economic approach was well established by the time Kennedy took office, the economic scene itself had been and was continuing to change. No longer were there the distinct priorities of a war or peace economy. Civil rights was the big domestic issue, but programs at home were constantly being tripped up by the Berlin Wall crisis, by the Bay of Pigs fiasco, by the growing involvement in Southeast Asia, all of which made for a blending of the economics of peace and war.

Riding the wave of remorse following Kennedy's assassination came Lyndon Johnson. That wave of feeling plus Johnson's talents as a political oarsman put many of Kennedy's reform projects up onto the beach at last. Victory was sweet, but of short duration. Almost unnoticed, the conflict in Southeast Asia was building. Flushed with confidence, Johnson saw himself moving the welfare state to triumph in both peace and war, the same sort of overextension that had bled Britain during the first half of this century.

Military expenditures for Vietnam and the domestic commitment to the "Great Society" rose side by side. More than ever before, the economy was pinched, not pushed on, by the war. Cutbacks in domestic spending were inevitable. Once again, the war was not large enough for direct economic controls such as rationing, but the United States balance-of-payments relationship with Europe, which had tilted in Europe's favor during the Korean War, was now so dangerously out of balance that doubts were being raised as to the dollar's stability as international currency. The specter of Truman's Korean War had returned in the Vietnam War to haunt Johnson, and he had the dignity to resign from the political contest. Once again the nation selected a President they hoped would be a Republican peacemaker.

Government–Business Relations   Whether at peace or war, the process of war involvement that began with Wilson and the First World War and grew with Roosevelt and the second, has shown no abatement in recent years. It has made for increasingly big and permanently established government. This growth in government, of course, has not been limited to the area of international activity. The nature of the government's role in business has changed and expanded, too. The great fear before Wilson was that the state would become a tool of business, giving tax benefits and tariff help, with congressmen responding to massive campaign contributions and serving as spokesmen for their local corporations. The early response of government in this relationship was negative, and restrictive measures such as antitrust legislation were invoked.

More recently, government has assumed a positive stance, giving tax subsidies to corporations as well as FHA mortages for housing. It has also financed education and manipulated money to control depressions. A growing fear that the state would dominate business entirely, a fear present especially during the early New Deal period, has subsided. Today, the government underwrites the largest capital commitments to private industry, primarily in defense production, in a way that leads to a blurring of the roles and interests of private capital and government.

Private capital may have lost personality since the days of the robber barons, but otherwise it has grown along with government. Today there are over 12 million distinct business enterprises in the United States. They are graded in size from General Motors, which is really an international business, down to the organ-grinder and his monkey. But of these millions, should the largest 100 be eliminated, telephones would go dead, trains and trucks would almost cease to run, and the country would be without heat, light, or the means of defense, a disaster beyond contemplation.

The last big attack by the Supreme Court on monopolies took place in 1911 with the breaking up of the Standard Oil Company. Traditionally, monopoly has had a bad name and has been prohibited in isolated cases, but more and more the entire economy is taking on the nature of a monopoly. The old test of guilt was an overt agreement as to prices, but more recently the Supreme Court has held that a mere tacit understanding between alleged competitors was sufficient indication of guilt. If, in fact, this test were rigorously applied, almost every large company in the United States would be dragged into court.

This lack of competitive procedure is not the result of conspiracy, but of natural change. Since World War II, big business has regained much of the prestige it lost during the depression years. The greatest number of companies and the most avid competition usually exist in the beginning states of the development of a new business area. This has been true of oil and steel in the late nineteenth century, of radios and automobiles in the twentieth, of television after World War II. The process is automatic, for only when a business is new is entry easy. Then all are small and many can share. Gradually competition narrows. Under the classic theory, the only alternative to a monopoly is active competition, but the trend today is for a few big corporations to share a market. When this occurs, whether in tobacco, chemicals, or what-have-you, the situation is called an oligopoly. There is little alternative. The days of Franklin, even of Edison, are gone. Invention is becoming costly and sophisticated, and only wealthy companies can afford the research, technical equipment, and cost of developing innovations.

Where an oligopoly exists and the goods and services offered are very nearly a complete substitute for one another, a uniformity of prices tends to occur. Should this price uniformity result from an explicit agreement, a cartel is formed. A cartel is illegal in the United States, but a similar result is achieved by what is usually called "price leadership." This is what occurs when one leading company adjusts its prices as a signal to the others. Actual competition would be ruinous. Like so many mice around a cheese, small concerns can afford to compete, but when tigers begin to fight, the result is economic war that may devastate the whole community. In a system of individual entrepreneurs, a man squeezed out of one market might try another, but with the huge, complex companies of today, changeover is so difficult and expensive as to be almost impossible.

As business has grown and changed, so has labor. It has had to in order to survive. Initially, against the robber barons, the fight was carried on more often than not with sticks and stones. Later, as the government became concerned with limiting monopoly in the sale of goods, it made no move against what might be viewed as monopoly in the sale of labor services by growing unions. Formerly, any association of workers had been regarded as a subversive plot against the public interest, and each worker had been obliged to bargain as he pleased, which usually meant take what he was offered or starve. Under the New Deal, the court injunction was occasionally used against labor to prevent strikes. In 1935 the Wagner Act created the National Labor Relations Board to supervise the settlement of disputes. After World War II, the Taft-Hartley Act recognized the legitimacy of labor unions and laid down what were to be considered unfair practices by both employer and labor union. Freedom of labor from charges of monopoly has led to industry-wide bargaining and to pressures that force up wages and subsequently prices. Strikes in many areas have become a threat to public safety and health.

From embattled outcast, labor has moved toward a position in the establishment. No longer are labor and business directly at odds. More often there is a grudging acknowledgment of mutual interest in maximizing profits all around. While the entrepreneur would have fought unions with strong-arm squads, the mature corporation of today is more willing to trade profits for protection against such an undirected event as a strike. More and more, jobs that were once solely manual are becoming more technical. More education is required for them, and the worker is moving over from the so-called blue-collar area into that of the white-collar worker. To a certain extent, this tends to move his identification from labor to management.

While the lot of the average laboring man has improved enormously, a price has been and is being paid. One is not apt to find any more John Henrys ready to die to prove a hammer better than a steam drill, but labor still fears innovation. Superficially, technology seems to threaten present jobs, though in the long run more jobs are usually created. This was the case with the carriage builders who feared the coming of the automobile.

Another unfortunate tendency of big labor is to deny the concept of a "decent day's work." Labor tends to shift the emphasis from production to full employment, thus denying effort and enterprise their reward. An example was the novice wartime worker who assembled three times the usual number of bombsights during a night shift. Something had to be wrong, and the job foreman insisted that all the units be disassembled and searched for mistakes. None was found, but the new employee got the message.

The only workers who have maintained a semblance of old-time competition are the farmers. They can't afford research staffs like those in large industries, and they have left experimentation to the Department of Agriculture. In 1631, tobacco planters petitioned the crown for redress against unfair merchants. This appeal resulted in the first price-support pro-

CAPITALISM

gram, and ever since then farmers have had to rely on federal power for muscle. Not that they haven't tried for collective bigness. Toward the end of the nineteenth century the Grangers, an organization formed by midwestern farmers, tried to bring the railroads and warehouses under state control. Another device tried out between the world wars was the farmers' cooperative. Never a tight enough structure to have real market strength as far as selling is concerned, the co-op movement has proved a success in the field of passive purchasing.

Growing business, then, has led the way and the other economic forces have followed, more or less successfully. Whether the end result is bad or good, it certainly cannot be described as competitive capitalism of the traditional school. That has gone forever, but what remains is not necessarily disastrous. A novel and widely accepted description of the present situation has been offered by the economist John Kenneth Galbraith. Bigness clearly begets bigness. Big business brings big labor, big manufacturing makes for big retailers, and the government is the strengthening balance wheel.

The Theory of Countervailing Power Under the old formula, restraints on private power were seen as inherent in the market itself. That is, if a businessman overcharged his customers, they went to his competitor across the street. With that kind of competition gone, it is much easier for the surviving big producers tacitly to adjust prices. However, Galbraith predicts new restraints on economic tyranny. In place of competition, he has set his theory of countervailing powers. Take as an example the marketing of consumer goods: the larger retail stores depend on a volume of sales at low prices, and so must resist the demands of the wholesaler or lose out to the more intimate businesses that offer the personal touch at a slightly higher price. This need for countervailing power in marketing has led to the rise of variety chains, big mail-order houses, and food and department chain stores that have sufficient bargaining power to meet on an equal footing with the wholesalers. In the long run, according to an optimistic Galbraith, countervailing powers tend to work in the consumer's best interests. Certainly unrestrained primary power, exclusively in the hands of one interest group or the other, does not. The chief hazard is that power may fall into the hands of one particular group, forcing government involvement.

International Economic Relations As capitalism has changed on the national scene, on the international it has just as drastically altered. In 1580, the English historian Richard Hakluyt advised merchants dealing with poor countries to help in the enrichment of their soil so that they would have more raw materials to trade for finished products. Some governments did get involved and introduced the age of mercantile exploitation. With Adam Smith, mercantile attitudes yielded to free trade, a change that benefited the underdeveloped countries very little. More recently, the pendulum has again swung toward government involvement, a corollary of Keynesian manipulation to stabilize the economy. Consequently a more restrictive attitude of protectionism, with tariffs and trade restrictions, has developed in the last few years.

Regardless of theory or national policy, international capitalism has experienced enormous and very sophisticated growth in the twentieth century. A typical example is the development of the General Motors Corporation overseas. The company was formed in 1908; in 1911 one hundred Buicks, fully assembled, were shipped to foreign customers, but until the end of World War I, there was little demand for a worldwide motor-vehicle business. The 1920s brought to the United States the age of the Tin Lizzie. Europe lagged behind, and protective tariffs made it prohibitively expensive to ship fully assembled vehicles at a profit. However, the shipping of parts could be undertaken at lower tariff rates, and this had the added advantage of making it possible to tailor features to local taste.

General Motors began setting up field offices abroad. The next step was to establish overseas assembly facilities to provide a basis for international growth and long-term commitment. An obvious progression from assembly was actual manufacturing. Since the home demand for cars was pressing, trained technicians and labor could not be spared, so, rather than build facilities, established factories were purchased: Vauxhall Motors in England as of 1925, and Germany's Opel works four years later. Timing was bad. With the depression, the operation became at best a holding one, and with the Second World War the Opel works were seized by the Nazis and subsequently battered by Allied bombers. The Vauxhall works also suffered war damage.

If production lagged, thinking ahead did not. In an example of capitalist planning and prognosis to put the communist economists to shame, the directors of General Motors had concluded in 1944 that within twenty years after the war the foreign automobile market would catch up with North American demand. Upon the basis of this forecast—correct within a year—decisions to restore the damaged plants were made. The basic principles of operation called for coordination through centralized staff functions but, more importantly, for the decentralization and adaptability that communism has had such trouble learning, and that are of first importance where different languages, money, business laws, and national traditions are involved.

Directly after the war, the world was starved for transportation. With Vauxhall and Opel again doing business, General Motors set up a plant in Australia, after determining that the market was promising and the government sympathetic. By the mid-fifties, demand in Australia and Europe was comparable to that of the United States in the 1920s. Meanwhile, accelerated industrialization was taking place in the underdeveloped countries, whether by socialist or capitalist means or by a combination of the two. It has long been popular to blame a lagging economy on international exploitation. In Latin America, the United States was the usual target, but although the United States—or U.S. business enterprises—had often taken excessive profits and shipped them home, they did not depend on this exploitation for survival, as Marx suggested, nor was it of such a nature as to entirely hold back local economy.

Since the Second World War, however, the situation has changed drastically. With cold-war competition for allies, it has become more common for wealthy governments to pour funds back into the underdeveloped nations, and the role of international capitalism has become a most delicate and demanding one. Most developing countries want to build cars as a matter of government policy, and they want the building to be a local matter. Thus, duties have been raised on imports. Usually, with the market small, manufacturers remain small.

An example was Argentina, where before World War II General Motors found an eager market. Since the war, Argentina has moved toward local manufacture. Because of the relatively small market, it would better serve General Motors to import parts and simply assemble them in Argentina, but, thanks to tariff policies, this would result in the price of a car being many times that of a locally made vehicle. Only a very few of Veblen's conspicuous consumers would be attracted to such a purchase. Consequently, GM had to set up complete manufacturing facilities in Argentina, which functioned as an integral part of the country's economic life. Employees paid by the hour were all locally recruited, and the higher staff positions were increasingly held by citizens. In 1971 the government's resistance to foreign-run business caused the plant to be shut down, but similar arrangements still operate harmoniously in Mexico, Brazil, and in the Republic of South Africa.

General Motors is a typical example of a nongovernmen-

CAPITALISM

tal industrial empire becoming internationalized with interests invested far beyond the purely explosive ones of a century past. The old "apparatus of Western imperialism," in Soviet terminology, required only merchants and a government with the power and the will to conquer overseas territory where needed. Today, international cooperation in one form or another is required.

For a planned international economy, Europe has developed a cartel pattern, which the United States has frowned on as a restraint of competition. Still, it has worked. This system is exemplified by the European Coal and Steel community, which is a semisovereign, supranational body capable of planning Western European coal and steel production unobstructed by national barriers. Practical big business is not compatible with the strangulation effect of a multiplicity of tariffs. This particularly applies to modern Europe, with its many small nations. Either business, industrial, and banking groups must cross national lines with the cooperation of governments or they must turn over these arrangements to the governments themselves. In the past, governments have never proved as successful as businessmen in making such economic agreements, and thus far Europe has swung to internationally guided capitalism in preference to international socialism.

It is with such international groups that overseas American businesses must deal. Very often they have dealt with the foreign governments directly, and difficult questions have arisen when the foreign government has engaged in policies adverse to American business interests. Normally, the Department of State will support American businessmen, and it will often press for concessions, especially when a business is operating under old and oppressive agreements. A case in point has been the negotiation of a fairer distribution of profits between Venezuela and American oil companies that the Venezuelan government has been threatening to nationalize. In former times, such companies sometimes tried to control foreign governments, as with Nicaragua in the nineteenth century, but since the Second World War these manipulations have generally proved too risky. Business abroad has largely swung away from involvement in local politics, despite pressure to contribute to the campaign funds of local political groups.

In some areas, large capitalist corporations have almost approximated a functioning world economic government. Notable for its scope and early formation was the "As Is" agreement regarding oil. In 1926 there existed a balance of power in oil markets due to an arrangement between the seven biggest companies operating from the Dutch East Indies to Iran. While governments watched nervously, a price war developed and spread worldwide with ruinous results until, in 1928, negotiations resulted in the "As Is" agreement. This amounted to a commercial peace treaty and economic world government for oil, with market areas set out. An association of these oil companies was formed to assess world demand, allocate quotas, and pool tankers not otherwise being used. By United States standards, this would seem a criminal restraint of trade. To others, it was simple common sense. The Sherman antitrust law was unenforceable on a worldwide scale, so it took the depression to disrupt the "As Is" agreement. It has never been restored, but commerce in oil has continued to demonstrate great worldwide cooperation.

This cooperation was tested to the extreme in the early 1950s when Iran seized installations of the Anglo-Iranian Oil Company, a predominantly British concessionary corporation. By the time the dispute was resolved, the Iranian share of the world market had been absorbed by other suppliers. In 1954, three European and five American oil companies met and agreed to market a part of the Iranian oil, and thereby Iran was returned to the world market.

The variety and sheer volume of twentieth-century production makes economic isolation impossible. Every country needs or wants what other countries have. It is no longer practical to seize property. Economic cooperation is required, and this knowledge is present at every council table, whether it be the board of directors of General Motors, the President and his cabinet, or the military chiefs of staff. Whether one regards this situation as good or bad, it is an unavoidable fact in a shrinking world. To date, the big companies have thrived outside their own borders and, if they have not resolved the questions of international survival, they have kept up with them.

Although the United States government has remained supervisory regarding international private capital, there is an area of economic importance where its role has grown enormously since World War II. In 1944, at Bretton Woods, the World Bank and International Monetary Fund were born. Their concern at the time was the reconstruction of Europe, a task that proved overwhelming. The Marshall Plan, though too much a tactical weapon in the struggle with Russia, filled the breach. As the European situation stabilized and prospered, the machinery of relief was redirected to the vastly more complex problems of the underdeveloped world.

Even before the Second World War, the universality of the 1929 depression had attested to worldwide economic interdependence. To ignore the economic fate of one's neighbors is to export poverty. No nation can prosper in isolation, and neglecting to export prosperity is eventually to import hard times. Today there is no doubt about the need of much of the world. Populations are growing, often faster than the minuscule economies of their countries. While expectations rise, poverty increases, and it becomes the self-protective duty of prosperous countries to help out. Ideally, this should result from coordination of trade policies and a sharing between industrial nations. Good results have already been achieved by international assistance to Formosa and Israel, both relatively small and energetic countries. But larger problems still exist, none larger than that of India. While many countries have surpluses of food, India has starvation. The United States has sent some food surpluses there, but that constitutes only a drop in a leaky bucket. Ideally, there should be some world market for available surplus, coupled with major efforts to encourage self-help and to discourage the use of profits for purposes alien to agriculture.

The problem of rehabilitating underdeveloped countries, a challenge to modern capitalism, socialism, and communism alike, is immense and still largely unexplored. It cannot be avoided. The industrialized nations must serve as combined diplomat-investors, showing the way to allocate resources and aid effectively. The process must begin with hard questions. Is a certain location appropriate for construction of a dam? If so, is there a present or future need for a dam there? Can the local economy be bolstered by some other means? All this calls for planning and a balancing of growth against the demands that growth must serve. Such help is unavailing unless some preconditions are met by the needy country. The government must be stable. There must be an educational establishment to cope with an increasingly technical way of life. There must be economic innovators to apply funds and expand trade to the point that the increasing ability of the public to consume mass-produced goods has the strength to break the shackles of a heretofore survival economy. Hopefully, in the end, that process will become self-sustaining. In any event, it is a massive challenge to international capitalism and to the governments of the industrialized Western world.

Conclusion: Today and Tomorrow

It has already been seen how modern capitalism, for its own preservation, tends toward a balance among its traditionally competitive members, and how other economically powerful units such as government and labor have grown to meet its challenge. This tendency toward protective cooperation has also been evidenced in the fast-growing international business community. Apart from the Communist-dominated countries, a condition of relative capitalistic freedom exists today throughout the world, with more or less governmental interference depending on the extent to which each government professes socialism.

The robber barons have left the stage: the Morgans, the Fricks, the Carnegies. In their place is a faceless management whose directors have the pcwer to do society great harm. Although most big companies are owned by stockholders, the stockholders have no practical influence on a corporation's conduct. The more than three million shareholders of American Telephone and Telegraph, for instance, could not possibly run such an enterprise effectively, but in the aggregate they represent massive economic power. That power is in the hands of the board of directors: power to use the money that the part owners have invested, and power to influence society at large in the process. All that each actual owner retains is a right to withhold his support from the management, a modified right to receive a part of the profits, and the right to sell his stock for cash.

This leaves the modern corporation executive in a position somewhat like that of the great fifteenth-century Florentine banker Cosimo de' Medici, who, without depending upon holding public office, ran his small country, subsidized artists, and, thanks to his wisdom, became a spark and sponsor of the Italian Renaissance. Unfortunately, not all modern businesses take their public role as seriously as did the Medici family. Though big business likes to pose as the servant of the people, television's puffing of shoddy products in fancy packaging suggests the real story. Scarcely in the public's interest was an aircraft company's taking nearly 50 percent profits on defense contracts, and the manner in which directors and top executives vote one another salaries in the neighborhood of half a million dollars a year has become so commonplace as to warrant scarcely a raised eyebrow.

Fortunately there are restraints. The most obvious is actually perhaps the least important—the action of stockholders. Theoretically, stockholders can vote out their management for poor performance, but most stockholders today have little connection with the great corporations whose stock they own. Though they receive annual reports and proxy notices indicating the management's suggested vote, stockholder revolts are rare, and successful ones almost unrecorded. More effective than in the days of the robber barons, however, is public opinion. Few corporate executives today feel they can afford to take positions in total disregard of public sentiment. Goodwill is a strong force, and general disapproval may not only cut sales but deprive directors of their positions. This happened in the case of an oil company president who, just before the Second World War, was found selling petroleum by a roundabout route to Nazi Germany.

Opinion from within also counts. An executive is bound to become identified with his firm. The question "Who are you with?" is to be taken as seriously, from the point of view of self-esteem, as "Who are you?" His and the company's image are one. As long as the executive is well salaried, it is not in his interest, as it was for many robber barons, to push profits mercilessly.

Despite the unequaled size of modern capitalism and the complacency of the American public regarding the practices of modern capitalism, this economic system has its prophets of doom. The first of these was Karl Marx. The capitalism against which he railed was not the capitalism of today. Where his doctrines flourish now, capitalism has vanished as a significant force, though it is not completely forgotten. A few years ago Nikita Khrushchev, then Soviet Premier, promised to bury capitalism, not with atomic bombs, but by the economic competition of his totalitarian form of socialism, or "state capitalism" as it has been called. Similar forecasts have come from within the system itself, notably from the respected economist Joseph Schumpeter. Schumpeter saw capitalism's downfall coming from its strengths, not its weaknesses. He predicted the entrepreneur would vanish and be replaced by monopolies. Indeed, this has in part occurred. With the entrepreneur's disappearance, Schumpeter thought the economic advantages that gave capitalism its appeal would also diminish, to be supplanted by government. The resulting system would be socialistic.

This expectation seemed nearer to the mark twenty years ago than it does today. American capitalism will, in time, undoubtedly change beyond recognition, as all economic systems have, but it is not apt to fall victim to other equally timeworn institutions. Since the Second World War, capitalist development has been unmatched, with the guiding assistance, rather than the encroachment, of government. If it has shown strains, so have its competitors. Democratic socialism made a surge in hard-pressed countries after 1945. Britain, particularly, tried a limited socialism and found that the difficult alternative to independent management was to move vast decision-making staffs into the civil service. Democratic socialism came with the promise of human transformation. An English novelist characterized socialism as Novocain for the soul. Now that the pain of World War II has subsided, the system has lost much of its appeal. Other countries that today rely on a socialist system are for the most part underdeveloped ones. In such preindustrial societies, a viable free-enterprise system has never had a chance to develop.

Communism is the other apparent threat to capitalism. It still has great appeal, but not, as Marx hypothesized, for industrially developed countries. As Lenin foresaw, it takes root more readily in emerging and backward nations. Some economists have been impressed by the growth rate of the USSR. Yet there are less costly ways to revitalize an economy than by a Bolshevik revolution, and, as that revolution recedes into the past, revisionism gains ground in Russia, along with a more comfortable, middle-class mode of life. The more men enjoy the world they have, the less they will risk losing it, and the less impatient they are to change that world at any price.

One's preference for capitalism or communism, in the final analysis, becomes a value judgment. Democratic capitalism assumes that healthy individuals make for a healthy group, while communism assumes that a healthy group makes for healthy individuals. In the democratic system, the state springs from society, while in the Soviet state the reverse is true. It is only an assumption that people prefer individual to group thinking and acting, but it is one deeply cherished in democratic societies. Strong government, particularly the totalitarian system called for by Communist state capitalism, may be benevolent, but there is always the risk of tyranny. Even democratic socialism is in danger of a hardening authoritarianism, a risk that seems not worth the running if democratic capitalism can achieve social security and economic stability.

Assuming that capitalism will survive into the foreseeable future, it will not exist in a static form. There are the challenges and the grinding wheels of world change to be faced. There are the worldwide capitalistic empires that, despite a governmental trend toward protective tariffs and restraints, seem destined to become more internationally involved. Such developments must serve not only the businesses themselves but also the countries of which they are becoming a part. The possible benefits, particularly to underdeveloped nations, are employment, training in advanced technology, and the infusion of capital. To survive, these world businesses must be good citizens wherever they operate, conforming to local laws and also respecting social and cultural traditions. Ideally, nationalistic barriers will break down and free trade prevail, with truly international ownership of big companies taking place. From the viewpoint of business, there is no barrier to worldwide ownership of shares. Unfortunately, today, overseas exchange restrictions and the probability of taxation on dividends in more than one country make any such free flow of investment prohibitive. Still, the possibility exists, and with worldwide economic sharing should come enhanced interest in keeping world peace.

Capitalism is an ongoing process. It thrives on change. The likelihood is that units will grow larger and will be balanced by enlarged government. Another path with attractions points toward what has been called a society of classless capitalists. With capital and labor confronting one another as they do today, the situation makes government involvement and heavy taxation necessary for a healthy distribution of wealth.

Classless capitalism, favored by some economists, would eliminate this confrontation. They see it as coming about through gradual diffusion of capitalists into the widest possible private ownership and through the reduction of the labor force by advancing automation and technology. Clearly such a change of direction would involve massive governmental efforts toward breaking up monopolies and protecting private property. Investment preferences would have to be granted to small or new capitalists, with income tax deterrents to personal concentration of wealth. This diffusion of wealth is not an impossible development, and on paper it has attractive features that undoubtedly will become more attractive as human labor gives way to automation.

Within the capitalist community there remains the question of poverty, that illness for which both communism and democratic socialism profess to offer healing medicine. Welfare has for years been capitalism's intended cure. The underprivileged remain a great problem that must be dealt with in both the private and public sectors. Should government with heavy taxes, often wastefully squandered by impersonal agencies, be solely responsible for the old, the ill, and the incompetent? Or should private charities, overlapping and inefficient, take over the field? To what extent does welfare discourage individual initiative? Questions are many and complex, yet of all capitalism's problems, poverty seems the least difficult. Hopefully, the enormous funds expended on armaments may soon be diverted to the domestic scene. Then the war on poverty may become a war in fact, with increased involvement on the part of government.

Another awesome problem is constant inflation, the so-called wage-price spiral. The Keynesian formula has proved more successful in the opposite direction, controlling depression. Keynes' remedy for inflation is increased taxes, decreased government spending, and restricted bank credit. In practice, more may be needed. One possibility is governmental price and wage controls, an extreme device that, until 1971, had been undertaken in the United States only in wartime.

Since World War II, the huge Pentagon building has dominated the Washington scene. There has been no real return to peace in terms of spending, for over $1,000 billion have gone for defense since the war. The image of the cold war, of implacable enemies in the world coupled with the international arms race, have made for a self-perpetuating mechanism. Short of massive reappraisals, there can be no end to such spending or to that slightly sinister phenomenon referred to as the military-industrial complex. Of course, this armaments spending has certain economic benefits. It creates a war economy without wartime loss, and, to this extent, massive government spending may be considered a Keynesian stimulant. Certainly the military is well fed in consequence, but dangers are obvious. The lesson of Krupp is not to be forgotten.

Military men may say they hate their profession, but it is through war that promotions, fame, and a purpose are made possible. Short of war itself, there is the perpetuation of the cold war with the ever-present hazard of outbursts, great and small. Finally, there is the increasing dependency of big business. Many firms, virtually existing on government contracts, would go bankrupt without them. Thousands would be unemployed, creating such an economic hazard that the government feels obliged to purchase simply to keep factories operating whether or not there is any need for the product. This effect has been most conspicuous in the case of certain aircraft manufacturers, where an example was provided of the self-perpetuating mechanism mentioned above: munitions for munitions' sake, with the company depending on government for funds, and the government not daring to put thousands out of work.

Such mutual dependency has other consequences. Where contracts involve classified material, companies have been forced into the position of firing employees as security risks in order to keep the contract. This amounts to a deprivation of liberty without benefit of due process of law. Although the Defense Department has formed a board to hear arguments on related issues, other government bureaus have lagged. There have also been cases where the companies themselves have independently undertaken security measures without the government being directly involved.

Another multifaceted problem of modern capitalism derives from what is generally regarded with satisfaction as our affluent society. Technology has made for more leisure hours than ever before. In time, this boon may become more of a problem than now seems possible. We are on the verge of the cybernetic age. During the Second World War, the navy first developed electronic devices to sense the approach of enemy airplanes and to direct guns toward them faster than any human possibly could. This principle of feedback of "sensory" impressions to automatic control machinery is gradually extending to the production line. Work hours will shrink, leaving in some cases both psychological problems due to enforced retirement and inactivity, and questions of guaranteeing incomes, and the like.

Another problem related to affluence in a free-enterprise system is the balancing of production between public and private sectors of the economy. Emphasis in the United States has increasingly been upon consumer goods, with each item creating the need for more. Cars demand gas and gas stations. Meanwhile, the public sector lags and vehicular construction moves out of line with road building. Packaged household goods are produced beyond the nation's capacity to remove the resulting trash. The consequence is that we drive in power-steered, air-conditioned vehicles through filthy potholed streets and littered cities, out past ranks of billboards, to picnic at last from hygienically packaged food beside a stream full of beer cans, bottles, and dead fish. Thus far, private industry has shown little response to the management of pollution, which in terms of diminished wildlife, squandered minerals, and poisoned atmosphere and waterways is far more than an aesthetic problem. It concerns the entire world, and if business does not energetically seek solutions, governments, including that of the United States, will inevitably have to take a direct lead.

In dealing with these emerging economic and political problems, the trend has been toward governmental planning. Economists have always favored planning on the part of individuals and private business, but not all of them have approved such activity on the international or national levels. Not that there isn't historical precedent. The mercantile age featured wide planning, but classical economists rejected its undertakings and insisted on absolute economic freedom. Today governments have grown in importance economically. Even if they do not directly manipulate prices and production, their policies regarding taxation and spending have brought significant consequences to the whole national economy. National governments have, as well, undertaken direct production of many goods and services.

Where planning has become anathema, it is chiefly because of its association with Soviet communism. It is part and parcel of the regularly announced five-year plans that have been used to push Soviet output to the limit. Trotsky favored it, as did Stalin, and it worked at considerable price in human suffering. That was during the early phases of coal and steel production, which required masses of unskilled labor. Its application to more sophisticated consumer production is dubious, and even the Soviet Union has begun to show a swing toward diversification of authority.

Governmental planning need not mean complete governmental ownership of the means of production, as is the case in Soviet Russia. While Soviet planning is largely political, other countries have worked out purely economic planning. Since before World War II, in western Europe governmental ownership has been more common than in the United States. Railways, bus services, in Germany partial operation of Volkswagen production, have been in governmental hands. Following the war, planning accompanied by the nationalization of major industries took place in Britain, with the emphasis on persuasion rather than coercion. In Sweden, where democratic socialism has been the dominant political form, planning has existed without the less savory corollary of nationalization.

Planning and/or nationalization of industry: have we either in the United States? Not long ago the question would have been answered with a shuddering, categorical negative. Even the present governmental role in minimizing economic fluctuation would have been frowned upon, with the explanation that the boom-or-bust cycle clears out deadwood. Then along came the Great Depression and Keynes. Ever since that time, governmental intervention to stabilize the economy has been a fact.

There is more to consider than simply momentary prosperity. In the future, there must be research to improve industrial methods, and education to provide skilled technicians to apply those methods. There must be constant investment to replace and expand public facilities such as roads, dams, school plants. All this is being undertaken by the government at the expense of the public's indulgence in luxury goods. This growth comes from taxation, which is rarely popular. Here Communist competitors have an advantage, for what they require for the public sector of their economy is never paid out to the public in the first place. Yet public expenditure must remain a problem in a free society, and unless it is well handled and made acceptable to the taxpayers, the United States may not fare well in the struggle for economic growth and national fulfillment.

The capacity to plan added to the power to effectuate that plan is the highest trust a democratic society can give to a statesman. If well executed, it need not become inconsistent with individual choice. It need not reduce the economic strength of big corporations. All that cooperative planning need amount to is the free agreement between private business and public government as to the desirability of economic goals for the future. To some extent this cooperation is already taking place. It may never be called planning as such, and it is unlikely to become coercive as in the Soviet model.

Even less foreseeable is the massive nationalization of private business, though this, too, has occurred in the case of stumbling facilities that are vital to the public interest, regardless of whether or not they make money. Typical are New York City's public housing projects, and its subway system. Throughout the nation railroads are in bad shape. They cannot be allowed to go bankrupt, nor can a private company perpetually run in the red and survive. In this case, the government must intervene with subsidies or even purchase and management. An example here is Amtrak, a corporation formed by congress in 1972 to provide railroad passenger service. Such eventualities are desirable only where necessary public services such as power, transportation, and the like are involved, and likely only when private companies prove themselves unequal to the task. Otherwise thanks to Keynes the government can largely limit its direct intervention while providing indirect guidance.

In times of national crisis, war, or depression, the government is compelled to indulge in less subtle planning. No modern nation can win a war by letting consumers' choices and the profit system have their way, for consumers do not personally purchase tanks or atomic submarines or rockets. The two world wars have taught this lesson. They have made for concerted planning, not only within the nation's industries but among sovereign nations on an international scale, a trend that cannot be avoided if humanity is ever to move toward the goal of one world.

While we ponder the heady possibility of planning at various levels, one fact must never be overlooked. The economic greatness of the United States is primarily the result of its individual capitalists, of their vitality, imagination, initiative, and their willingness to compete and take risks. All this might be stifled by a comprehensive national plan. Though room remains for setting goals in broad terms, for anticipating economic imbalance, the rigidity of a detailed plan would undoubtedly bring a loss in freedom and its attendant virtues at a price no democratic nation would be willing to pay.

Neither communism nor socialism with their economic planning are apt to overcome capitalism in the foreseeable future. Nor is the reverse likely. Some economists have worked out a convergence theory with a blending of the three. This is a possibility; but more than any economic theory, there remains one force for world change that will influence all three systems. As the feudal lord pondered the doings of the village merchant and longed for his wares, so our merchants of today attend to the pronouncements of science. Professional scientific experts are a new force in the world. While capitalism has long been accepted as an inescapable fact of economic life, it has never been a subject of loud moral enthusiasm. Science, on the other hand, arrived as the white hope of the twentieth century, with an impact for the future no less significant than the democratic yearning of the eighteenth century.

While political theories, be they democratic, communistic, socialistic, or whatever, are limited by political loyalties, science knows no such bounds. It is universal, and universally revered. The march of science is impersonally inevitable. Business is helpless before technology, and therein lies the prospect of change. To date, science has added to the momentum of capitalism; but just as the merchant class made obsolete the feudal lord who was charmed by the wares of the village, so science, over the long haul, promises to render capitalism, socialism, and communism obsolete. Communism has been regarded as a threat by capitalism for, however unattractive, it does offer an alternative. No such hostility is directed toward science, which works quietly from within. It works now at a time of great doubts in the world. Communism is fast running out of messianic purpose and is rapidly discovering that it cannot build a society if it fails to satisfy men's wants. At the same time, capitalism is recovering from its obsession with productivity and wondering about values over and above pure consumer affluence. Science may not have the answers, but, for good or bad, in the twentieth century it has the momentum to lead the way.

To where? It would be presumptuous to guess and as hopeless as it would have been for the medieval knight to try to construe the sounds of industry around him into the vast industrial nations of today. To pretend to know is to deny the truth. One can but hope for a future wiser than the past, where human aspirations may flower as they have not done before. This can be no more than a hope, and it would be folly to put confidence in any one economic theory, political party, class, church, or nation to bring it about. It will happen as a result of all these forces working together or against one another, with science providing the fuel, either to propel or to consume.

Definitions

Agricultural Adjustment Administration (AAA) A New Deal agency designed to reduce overproduction in agriculture and equalize the farmer's profits with those of the businessman.

Babbitt From George Babbitt, the leading character in Sinclair Lewis's book *Babbitt*. The name is now applied to all insensitive businessmen.

Cartel An association of business competitors in the same field formed to control the market and create monopolies. From the German *Kartell*.

Caveat emptor Latin for "Let the buyer beware," a commercial policy giving a buyer no protection against hidden defects in his purchase.

Colbertism Economic policy that favored monopolies in overseas trade. Named for the seventeenth-century French minister of finance.

Conservative Darwinism In economic terms, refers to theories that considered uncontrolled cutthroat capitalism as a proper demonstration of the natural survival of the fittest. *See also* Darwinism.

Countervailing power A contemporary theory that bigness in one economic area, such as industry, will breed bigness in competitive areas—labor, government, etc.

Darwinism The theories advanced by Charles Darwin (1809–1882) to explain the process of evolution in natural life. They were extended by others into political, economic, and sociological areas.

Economic planning First instituted as a formal policy by the Communist governments to set up future quotas for industrial and agricultural development. Such planning now takes place to some extent in socialist and capitalistic systems as well, although in less rigid forms.

Fascism A totalitarian and authoritarian political philosophy that considers the individual in every respect subordinate to the interests of the historical reality of the national state.

Federal Reserve System A United States banking system set up by the Federal Reserve Act of December 23, 1913, concentrating the banking resources of the country and providing an elastic currency.

Guild An association of men belonging to the same occupation. In medieval times merchant guilds regulated commercial activities and maintained privileges such as monopolies and freedom from tolls within the group. Merchant guilds were prominent in the eleventh century. Trade guilds did not appear until about three centuries later.

Hansa A Germanic term for the early merchant guild.

Hanseatic League A confederacy established in 1241 between certain northern German cities for mutual protection and profit. It grew until in the fifteenth century as many as 160 towns were involved and was finally destroyed (except for 6 member cities) in the Thirty Years War.

Hedonistic calculus According to the ancient Greek Aristippus, pleasure was the prime goal and end of man, and this philosophy was called hedonism after the Greek word *hedone,* meaning "pleasure." English philosopher Jeremy Bentham later made the concept into a formula under which man's daily activities were responsive to a balancing of pleasure versus pain, and this has been referred to as the hedonistic calculus.

Invisible hand In the economic terminology of Adam Smith, the underlying principle that assumes the optimum level of economic welfare of a society occurs when each member acts in his own self-interest.

Just price A concept developed by the early theological economists that held that the moral and just price of any product was the cost of the materials plus labor. The value of labor was to be determined on the basis of what the seller-manufacturer needed to maintain himself in his present way of life and employment. To charge more for a product was regarded as sinful.

Knights of Labor An American workmen's organization, founded in Philadelphia in 1869 and a pioneer in the labor movement.

Labor theory of value A theory initiated by the early classical economists that the value of an object depended upon the labor that went into its creation. This theory was later adapted by Karl Marx in his communist system of thought.

Laissez-faire French, literally "let do," an economic doctrine featuring a minimum of governmental regulation.

The leisure class, theory of An idea presented by Thorstein Veblen to the effect that capitalism produced a leisure class, the function of which was simply to display its wealth.

Malthusian law of population A doctrine advanced by T. R. Malthus, especially in *An Essay on the Principle of Population* (1798), holding that population increases faster than the food supply, so that if no check is put upon the process only starvation will act as a corrective.

Marginal utility theory This concept assumes that a purchaser will pay less the more he obtains of a desired object. The last object purchased, called the marginal item, sets the limit on a purchaser's demand and thereby sets a limit pricewise on the entire purchase. This quite laborious formula was prepared by the neoclassicists in order to support their laissez-faire theories against Marxist distortions of the old labor theory of value.

Mercantilism Economic policies determined by national rather than local or individual aims to build up national strength through a favorable balance of trade.

Military-industrial complex A term for the relationship of interdependence between the military and certain large industrial firms and the commercial production that results.

Monopoly In economics, the complete domination of a product or service market by a single firm.

National Recovery Administration (NRA) An administration set up by Franklin Roosevelt to inspire federal and industrial cooperation in the interest of priming the lagging economy.

Nazi Hitler's National Socialist German Workers' party. Nazi is the popularized contraction from *Nationalsozialist*.

Neoclassical economics This refers to economic theories drawn up in the mid-nineteenth century revamping the ideas of Adam Smith and his followers.

Oligopoly A situation close to monopoly where the produce is controlled not by one but by a few big companies that act in tacit concert.

Physiocrats A French school of economics favoring natural economic laws.

Populists Members of an American political party organized in 1891 by labor and agricultural groups favoring popular control.

Progressive party An American political party formed in 1912 to support Theodore Roosevelt for President. It encouraged various reform measures, such as women's suffrage.

Reform Darwinism In economic terms, this doctrine's supporters insisted that society could be improved by improving the economic environment of the poor. This was in opposition to the conservative Darwinists, who believed in the economic survival of the fittest.

Robber barons A term applied to the often-ruthless American capitalists of the nineteenth century.

Say's Law of Markets An economic law suggesting that production and demand always achieve a balance.

Scab A worker who disregards a strike and goes to his job.

Schoolmen Theologians of the Middle Ages who lectured in monastic cloisters or cathedral schools, such as those founded by Charlemagne and his successors.

Sherman Antitrust Act An American law passed in 1890 making combinations in restraint of interstate or foreign commerce illegal.

Slaughterhouse Cases A group of cases decided in 1873 by the Supreme Court of the United States. The verdict stated that the police power of the states was not impaired by the Fourteenth Amendment and thus allowed the city of New Orleans to restrict the butchering industry in that city by means of stringent laws.

Statute of Monopolies A statute that, in 1624, invalidated all crown-granted monopolies in England except those for inventors' patents. It was the first such legislation.

Tennessee Valley Authority (TVA) A New Deal project for the reclamation of the Tennessee Valley. Government-run, socialistic in nature, the project worked so well that it survived where other New Deal institutions were declared unconstitutional.

The welfare state A concept first developed in England and more recently applied in the United States under which every citizen is provided with minimal financial support regardless of his contribution to the society.

Biographies

Adams, Charles Francis, Jr. (1835–1915): Scholar, attorney, and president of the Union Pacific Railroad. When Jay Gould drove him from this position in 1890 he turned to historical writing, much of which is devoted to discrediting capitalists of the Gould stamp.

Aquinas, Thomas (1225?–1274): Italian theologian and philosopher. His writings such as *Catena Aurea* and *Summa Theologica* dominated man's concept of the universe for centuries to follow.

Astor, John Jacob (1763–1848): Arriving from Germany Astor became one of the first tycoons. He made his fortune in beaver pelts in the Northwest after creating the American Fur Company in 1808. His empire stretched as far as the mouth of the Columbia River.

Baer, George Frederick (1842–1914): Attorney and capitalist of the old school. As President of the Reading Company, he arrogantly denied the rights of coal miners. This impass lead to the great strike of 1902, in which for the first time the strikers won public support.

Bentham, Jeremy (1748–1832): English philosopher and jurist. Main exponent of utilitarianism, which saw morality as the functioning of increasing pleasure and decreasing pain.

Brandeis, Louis Dembitz (1856–1941): Proponent of a liberal legal philosophy; author; attorney in a number of cases concerned with economic and social reform. Associate Justice of the U.S. Supreme Court, 1916–1939.

Bryan, William Jennings (1860–1925): Lawyer and politician; known as "the Commoner." Ran several times for President as a Democratic reformer. Won nomination for Wilson in 1912 and was secretary of state 1913–1915.

Carnegie, Andrew (1835–1919): Came from Scotland to the United States. Entered iron and steel business and achieved great success. Devoted his later years to distributing his wealth for the benefit of society.

Charlemagne (742–814): King of the Franks, victorious general, expert administrator, and patron of learning and the arts. He filled the vacuum left in Europe by the collapse of Rome and organized the Holy Roman Empire.

Colbert, Jean Baptiste (1619–1683): French minister of finance and near dictator under Louis XIV, he developed an economic policy remembered as Colbertism. Basic mercantilism, it involved the extension of trade, heavy protective tariffs, and the building up of state funds.

Coolidge, John Calvin (1872–1933): Thirtieth President of the United States (1923–1929). Governor of Massachusetts; vice-president under Harding, sworn in as President at Harding's death. Elected on his own in 1924.

Cooper, Peter (1791–1883): Financial genius and enlightened American capitalist. Among the financial backers of the Atlantic cable, Cooper is better remembered for his altruisms, chief among them Cooper Union in New York City for the advancement of art and science.

Croly, Herbert (1869–1930): Social philosopher and writer, Croly established and edited *The New Republic*. Published in 1909, his book *The Promise of American Life* had a profound effect upon political thinking, and in many ways anticipated the development of national socialism.

Dickens, Charles (1812–1870): English novelist. As a child, he worked in a blacking factory, among other jobs, and many of his books were a protest against the social effects of selfish capitalism. Among them are *Oliver Twist, A Christmas Carol, Hard Times,* and *David Copperfield.*

Drew, Daniel (1797–1879): American financier; began as cattle drover, went into the steamboat and railroad businesses, and manipulated stock on Wall Street, where he was feared and respected as the "Great Bear."

Eisenhower, Dwight David (1890–1969): Commander-in-chief of Allied forces in Western Europe during the Second World War. President of Columbia University and later President of the United States (1953–1961).

Ely, Richard Theodore (1854–1943): Educator and economist. He taught political economics at Johns Hopkins, the University of Wisconsin, and Northwestern University. Ely sympathized with the working man and was influenced by Germany's welfare state to advocate an economic policy remembered now as reform Darwinism.

Fisk, James (1834–1872): Remembered as "Big Jim" and "Jubilee Jim," Fisk was an unprincipled stock-market manipulator. Hated by many for his milking of the Erie Railroad and his efforts to grab the gold market in 1869, his untimely demise came from another quarter, when he was shot down in a quarrel over a woman.

Ford, Henry (1863–1947): Automobile manufacturer who developed the production-line system. During World War I, chartered a "peace ship" to try to organize a peace conference to end the war.

Franklin, Benjamin (1706–1790): Statesman, scientist, printer, writer, inventor, noted for his wise sayings printed in *Poor Richard's Almanack* published from 1732 until 1757.

Galbraith, John Kenneth (1908–   ): American economist, professor, author of books on economics.

George, Henry (1839–1897): American economist; as a young man was a sailor and a typesetter. Wrote *Progress and Poverty* (1877–1879). Ran twice for mayor of New York and during his second campaign in 1897 was stricken with apoplexy and died.

Gould, Jay (1836–1892): American capitalist. Took over control of the Erie Railroad from Cornelius Vanderbilt and then the Union

Pacific, manipulating all his operations for his own personal aggrandizement.

Hakluyt, Richard (1552?–1616): English geographer, archdeacon of Westminster, member of Virginia Company of London. Wrote *Principall Navigations, Voiages, and Discoveries of the English Nation* (1589).

Harding, Warren Gamaliel (1865–1923): Twenty-ninth President of the United States (1921–1923); conservative Republican; against League of Nations; undermined by corrupt officials and died mysteriously while on speaking tour in San Francisco.

Henry, John: Legendary railroad worker who won a steel-driving contest against a machine and died of the strain.

Hindenburg, Paul von (1847–1934): German field marshal in World War I, and in 1925 elected president of Germany. Forced by Nazi party to appoint Hitler chancellor.

Hitler, Adolf (1889–1945): Austrian-born soldier in World War I. Politician; leader of Nazi party in Germany, finally dictator of all Germany from 1933 to 1945. In defeat during World War II, he killed himself.

Hoover, Herbert Clark (1874–1964): Thirty-first President of the United States (1929–1933). Mining engineer. Directed various economic measures in Europe during period following the armistice that ended World War I. President during the Great Depression.

Keynes, John Maynard (1883–1946): English economist. Represented the British treasury at the Paris Peace Conference in 1919. Author of many books on economics, and probably the most influential economist of the twentieth century, encouraging government involvement in economic activity.

Krupp von Bohlen und Halbach, Alfried (1907–1967): Son of Gustav Krupp, Alfried directed the Krupp factories during World War II, was convicted of war crimes and imprisoned from 1948 to 1951, when he went back to managing the firm.

Krupp von Bohlen und Halbach, Gustav (1870–1950): Husband of Bertha Krupp, whose name he received by marriage. German industrialist who during the formative years of the Nazi regime ran the great Krupp factory complex and gave complete support to Hitler. He died before he could be tried for his war activities.

Locke, John (1632–1704): Lecturer and philosopher. Known as father of British empiricism, which emphasized the important role of human experience. His *Essay concerning Human Understanding* was published in 1690.

Long, Huey Pierce (1893–1935): Lawyer and politician. Governor of Louisiana from 1928–1931. U.S. senator from 1931 until 1935, when he was assassinated. Though popular with Louisiana's poor people, he ruled there like a dictator.

Luther, Martin (1483–1546): German religious reformer. Preached salvation by faith rather than by deeds. Began organizing a Protestant church.

Machiavelli, Niccolò (1469–1527): Italian political philosopher and statesman. His most famous work was *The Prince,* containing his theory of government and suggesting cold-blooded devices for gaining and retaining power.

Malthus, Thomas Robert (1766–1834): English economist responsible for the widely held opinion that, while population increases geometrically, food increases only arithmetically.

Medici, Cosimo I de' (1519–1574): Known as "Cosimo the Great"; titled the duke of Florence, he ruled capably but despotically.

Mill, John Stuart (1806–1873): English philosopher and economist. Began as a follower of Bentham but drifted from this position, as well as from a more classical view of economics, to a more idealistic and socialistic viewpoint.

Mitchell, John (1870–1919): American labor leader; president of the United Mine Workers from 1898–1908. Led the anthracite coal strike of 1902.

Morgan, John Pierpont (1873–1913): Financier and banker. Reorganized major American railroads and helped finance the government from 1873. Collected many art treasures and became president of New York City's Metropolitan Museum of Art and a benefactor of the New York Public Library.

Mun, Thomas (1571–1641): English economist, director of the East India Company, and definer of theory of balance of trade.

Mussolini, Benito (1883–1945): Italian journalist, Socialist, and founder and leader of the Fascist party from 1921. Took over Italian government as dictator; conquered Ethiopia in 1936; brought his country to ruin in World War II, and was assassinated by Italian partisans.

Newton, Sir Isaac (1642–1727): English mathematician and natural philosopher. He conceived the idea of universal gravitation and saw nature operating subject to laws that economists would later interpret for use in their own field.

Powderly, Terence Vincent (1849–1924): American labor leader. Tried to harmonize disagreements between Knights of Labor and American Federation of Labor; mayor of Scranton, Pa. (1878–1884). U.S. commissioner general of immigration (1897–1902).

Quesnay, François (1694–1774): French economist and physician. Physician to the king of France and a formulator of the economic theory of the Physiocrats.

Ricardo, David (1772– 1823): English economist. Developed theory of rent, profit, and wages. A founder of classical school of economics.

Rockefeller, John Davison (1839–1937): American oil magnate. In 1870, organized Standard Oil Company and had oil monopoly until the Standard Oil Trust was dissolved in 1892 by court decree. Later founded charitable corporations including the Rockefeller Foundation and the Rockefeller Institute for Medical Research.

Roosevelt, Franklin Delano (1882–1945): Born into an old New York family, he became President (1933–1945) at the depths of the depression. Began many controversial economic programs; led country through most of World War II.

Roosevelt, Theodore (1858–1919): High-spirited champion of the "little man," President 1901–1909. Brought about progressive reforms of big business. Franklin D. Roosevelt was his distant cousin.

Ruskin, John (1819–1900): English art critic and sociological writer. Advocated national system of education; wrote essays to workmen and laborers on remedies for poverty and misery.

Say, Jean Baptiste (1767–1832): French economist and author of many important books in the field. Innovator of Say's Law of Markets.

Schumpeter, Joseph Alois (1883–1950): German economist; professor at Harvard and author of books on economics including, in 1939, *Business Cycles.*

Smith, Adam (1723–1790): Scottish economist. Professor at Glasgow

University; best remembered for his influential study *Inquiry into the Nature and Causes of the Wealth of Nations* (1776) which laid foundation for the science of political economy.

Spencer, Herbert (1820–1903): English philosopher. Influenced by Darwin's *Origin of Species* (1859). His writings encouraged economists to view economics as subject to the same natural laws of selection and survival as occur among living species.

Steffens, Lincoln (1866–1963): Editor, author, known as a muckraker for his exposures of corruption in business and government.

Sumner, William Graham (1840–1910): American sociologist and economist. Wrote numerous books and held the position that business flourished best when left to its own devices.

Tarbell, Ida Minerva (1857–1944): Author, employed by *McClure's Magazine,* which presented in 1904 her exposition of business practices, *History of the Standard Oil Company.*

Truman, Harry S. (1884–   ): Thirty-third President of the United States (1945–1953); formerly a U.S. senator and vice president. Developed the Marshall Plan to aid European economic recovery after World War II.

Turgot, Anne Robert Jacques (1727–1781): Turgot was the French controller general of finance under Louis XVI. A disciple of François Quesnay, Turgot undertook to introduce mercantile reforms based on what he regarded as natural economic laws, which envisioned no borrowing and no increase in taxation.

Vanderbilt, Cornelius (1794–1877): American capitalist who began with a ferry business between Staten Island and New York, and went on to obtain controlling interest in several railroad lines, accumulating a great personal fortune.

Veblen, Thorstein Bunde (1857–1929): American teacher and social scientist. His writings, attacking social and economic institutions, include his *Theory of the Leisure Class.*

Warburg, Paul Moritz (1868–1932): German banker and economist who was brought to the United States to help the reorganization of national banking just prior to World War I. During the war years (1914–1918) he was a member of the First Federal Reserve Board, correctly predicted the panic of 1929.

Wilson, Thomas Woodrow (1856–1924): Twenty-eighth President of the United States (1913–1921). Teacher, president of Princeton University (1902 –1910), reformer, advocate of League of Nations.

Biographies   **121**

Bibliography of Sources

Aron, Raymond. *The Industrial Society*. New York: Praeger, 1967.

Ashton, Thomas. *An Economic History of England: The Eighteenth Century*. New York: Barnes & Noble, 1955.

Berle, Adolf A., Jr. *The Twentieth-Century Capitalist Revolution*. New York: Harcourt Brace & World, 1954.

Bjork, Gordon C. *Private Enterprise and Public Interest*. Englewood Cliffs, N.J.: Prentice-Hall, 1969.

Black, Eugene R. *The Diplomacy of Economic Development*. Cambridge, Mass.: Harvard University Press, 1960.

Cantril, Hadley. *The Psychology of Social Movements*. New York: John Wiley & Sons, 1951.

Donner, Frederic G. *The World-wide Industrial Enterprise*. New York: McGraw Hill, 1967.

Durant, Will. *The Age of Faith*. New York: Simon and Schuster, 1950.

———. *The Reformation*. New York: Simon and Schuster, 1957.

———. *The Renaissance*. New York: Simon and Schuster, 1953.

Durant, Will, and Durant, Ariel. *The Age of Reason Begins*. New York: Simon and Schuster, 1961.

Fine, Sidney. *Laissez Faire and the General-Welfare State*. Ann Arbor, Mich.: University of Michigan Press, 1964.

Flynn, John T. *The Roosevelt Myth*. Rev. ed. New York: The Devin-Adair Co., 1956.

Friedman, Milton, and Schwartz, Anna Jacobson. *A Monetary History of the United States, 1867–1960*. Princeton, N.J.: Princeton University Press, 1963.

Fusfeld, Daniel R. *The Age of the Economist*. New York: William Morrow & Company, 1968.

Galbraith, John Kenneth. *The New Industrial State*. Boston: Houghton, Mifflin Co., 1967.

————. *American Capitalism*. Boston: Houghton, Mifflin Co., 1956.

Gilbert, G. H. *The Psychology of Dictatorship*. New York: Ronald Press Co., 1950.

Goldman, Eric F. *Rendezvous with Destiny*. New York: Alfred A. Knopf, 1952.

Hadley, Arthur T. *Power's Human Face*. New York: Garden City Books, 1958.

Hazlitt, Henry, ed. *The Critics of Keynesian Economics*. Princeton, N. J.: D. Van Nostrand Co., 1960.

Heilbroner, Robert L. *The Limits of American Capitalism*. New York: Harper & Row, 1966.

Hobson, John A. *Imperialism: A Study*. Ann Arbor, Mich.: University of Michigan Press, 1965.

Janeway, Eliot. *The Economics of Crisis: War, Politics, and the Dollar*. New York: Weybright & Talley, 1968.

Josephson, Matthew. *The Robber Barons*. New York: Harcourt Brace & World, 1962.

Kelso, Louis O., and Adler, Mortimer J. *The Capitalist Manifesto*. New York: Random House, 1958.

Kirkland, Edward. *Industry Comes of Age*. New York: Holt, Rinehart & Winston, 1961.

Legislative Reference Service. *Fascism in Action*. Washington, D.C.: U.S. Government Printing Office, 1947.

Lynch, Matthew J., and Raphael, Stanley S. *Medicine and the State*. Springfield, Ill.: Charles C. Thomas, 1963.

Means, Gardiner C. *The Corporate Revolution in America*. New York: Collier Books, 1964.

Moley, Raymond. *The First New Deal*. New York: Harcourt Brace & World, 1966.

Neale, Allan D. *The Antitrust Laws of the United States of America: A Study of Competition Enforced by Law*. Cambridge, England: Cambridge University Press, 1960.

Paton, William A. *Shirtsleeve Economics*. New York: Appleton-Century-Crofts, 1952.

Patterson, Ernest M. *An Introduction to World Economics*. New York: Macmillan Company, 1947.

Prochnow, Herbert V., ed. *World Economic Problems and Policies*. New York: Harper & Row, 1965.

Rand, Ayn. *Capitalism: The Unknown Ideal*. New York: The New American Library, 1966.

Roll, Erich. *A History of Economic Thought*. 3rd ed. Englewood Cliffs, N.J.: Prentice-Hall, 1956.

Rostow, Eugene V. *Planning for Freedom*. New Haven, Conn.: Yale University Press, 1959.

Schumpeter, Joseph. *Capitalism, Socialism, and Democracy*. 3rd ed. New York: Harper & Brothers, 1950.

Singer, Leslie. *Economics Made Simple*. New York: Garden City Books, 1958.

Soule, George. *The Ideas of the Great Economists*. New York: New American Library, 1955.

Stark, Werner. *The Ideal Foundations of Economic Thought*. New York: Oxford University Press, 1944.

Von Mises, Ludwig. *The Anti-Capitalistic Mentality*. Princeton, N. J.: Van Nostrand Co., 1956.

Ward, Barbara. *The Rich Nations and the Poor Nations*. New York: W. W. Norton & Co., 1962

Wilkins, Hughel, and Friday, Charles. *The Economists of the New Frontier*. New York: Random House, 1963.

Index

Damodar Valley, India, 59
Danube River, 9
Darcy v. Allein, 38
Darrow, Clarence, 46
Darwinism, 30
De Gaulle, Charles, 80
Democratic party (United States), 56, 78, 81
Democratic socialism, 4, 5, 67, 98
Denver Pacific Railroad, 32
Dewey, Thomas, 78
Dickens, Charles, 27
Drew, Daniel, 28, 30, 35

East India Company, 13
Economic Consequences of the Peace, The (Keynes), 61
Education, 66
Egypt, 81
Eisenhower, Dwight D., 81
Elizabeth I, Queen, 38
Ely, Richard, 42
England, *see* Great Britain
Erie Railroad, 32
European Coal and Steel community, 91
Exploitation, 13, 15

Fair Deal, 80
Fair Labor Standards Act, 60
Fairs, 9
Fascism, 3-5, 48

Italian, 67-69
modern, 77
nature of, 69-70
Federal government
    Federal Reserve System, 50
    government-business relations, 83-87
    planning, 104-105
    Tennessee Valley Authority, 58-59
Federal Housing Authority, 83
Federal Reserve Act, 50
Federal Reserve Banks, 81
Federal Reserve System, 50
Feudalism, 8, 11
Field, Stephen J., 37
Fisk, James, 30, 32
Florence, Italy, 10, 11
Food surpluses, 93-94
Ford, Henry, 51-52
Formosa, 93
France
    antimercantilism, 15-16
    French Revolution, 21
    Great Britain and, 17
    mercantilism, 13-14
    postwar economy, 79-80
Frankfurt, Germany, 9
Franklin, Benjamin, 27
Free enterprise, natural law of, 19-21

Population, Malthusian law, 22

Populism, 41-43, 47

Poverty, 29-30, 39, 93, 100

Powderley, Terence, 41

Price and wage controls, 101

Prince, The (Machiavelli), 12

Progress and Poverty (George), 42

Progressive party (Bull Moosers), 48

Progressivism, 47, 48

Promise of American Life, The (Croly), 47

Protective tariffs, 28, 51

Protestant Reformation, 12

Public opinion, 96-97

Quesnay, François, 15-16

Racial discrimination, 29

Railroads, 29, 32-33

Reading Coal Company, 45

Reform Darwinism, 42-43, 48, 49

Renaissance, 11

Republican party (United States), 48-49, 81

Rerum novarum (Leo XIII), 39

Revisionism, 98

Rhine River, 9

Ricardo, David, 22-23

Robber Barons, 28, 30-36, 50, 85, 95

Rockefeller, John D., 30, 33-34, 35, 38, 46

Roman Catholic church, 11-12

Rome, Italy, 7, 8, 11

Roosevelt, Franklin Delano, 78
  New Deal, 55-60
  World War II, 65-66

Roosevelt, Theodore, 45, 47, 50
  New Nationalism, 48-49

Ruskin, John, 42

San Juan Hill, battle of, 50

Say, Jean Baptiste, 23, 61-62

Say's Law of Markets, 23, 60-62

Scabs, 44

Schoolmen, 8

Schumpeter, Joseph, 97

Science, 106-107

Self-interest, theory of, 19-20

Serfs, 8

Serra, Antonio, 13

Sherman Antitrust Act, 38-39, 50, 52

Slaughterhouse Cases, 36

Slavery, 15, 26-29

Smith, Adam, 18-21, 25, 30, 60, 61, 88

Social security, 66

Socialism, 3, 5, 67, 94, 106

Society for the Prevention of Cruelty to Animals (New York), 41

South Africa, Republic of, 77, 90

South Improvement Company, 34

Spain, 77

Spanish-American War, 43

Spencer, Herbert, 30

Stalin, Joseph, 103

Standard Oil Company, 34, 84

State capitalism, 97, 99

State government, 36-37

Statute of Monopolies, 38

Steam engine, 21

Steffens, Lincoln, 47

Stockholders, 95-96

Strength Through Joy movement, 73

Strikes
coal strike (1902), 43-46
legislation, 85

Sumner, William Graham, 30

Supply and demand, theory of, 20-21, 61-62

Sweden, governmental planning, 104

Taft, William Howard, 48-49

Taft-Hartley Act, 85

Tarbell, Ida, 47

Taxation, 28, 51, 63, 66, 80, 99, 104

Technology, 86, 100, 102, 106

Ten-hour law, 49

Tennessee Valley Authority, 58-59

Theory of Business Enterprise, The (Veblen), 47

Theory of the Leisure Class, The (Veblen), 46-47

Thyssen, Fritz, 73

Trotsky, Leon, 103

Truman, Harry S., 78

Trusts, 31, 46, 49

Turgot, Jacques, 16

Turkish empire, 15

Tycoons, 27-28, 47

Unemployment, 56, 62, 66

Union Pacific Railroad, 32

Union of Soviet Socialist Republics, 62, 98
governmental planning, 103

United Mine Workers, 44

United States
agriculture, 29, 57-58
Civil War, 28-29, 60
coal strike (1902), 43-46
Constitution, 25-26
depression (1873), 40-42
domestic reform, 49-52
Eisenhower administration, 81

About the Author

James D. Forman is a well-known author of books for young people, among them *Shield of Achilles, Ring the Judas Bell,* and *My Enemy, My Brother.* The last two titles were honored in the *Book World* Spring Book Festival in the year of their publication.

Mr. Forman is a graduate of Princeton University and Columbia University Law School. He has traveled widely in Europe, especially in Greece, a country that has served as background for a number of his books. Mr. Forman lives on Long Island.